'Lyr... and eleg..., this... but is a... d... ...nt of an unusual
f... w... ie... ...ing... ...i... ...d
...r... ...es... ...n'
...ween humans and the changed (and changing) natural world.'
Helen Mort, chair of Boardman Tasker Award judges

'This is the kind of beautiful writing that transcends form –
in this case nature writing – to arrive somewhere improbable
and compelling.' Paul Evans, *Guardian*

'[Nicholson] chronicles walks on which he seeks it out under
cliffs and crags, in clefts and corries, and ponders its meaning.
A glorious little book.' Michael Kerr, *Daily Telegraph*

'This ravishingly lovely book is about thought-snow, summer snow,
flight, falling, stillness, memory, loss, mountains . . . An enigma and
an enchantment, beautifully observed and exquisitely written.
I was entranced and like Nicholson with his summer snow,
did not want to let it go.' Keggie Carew, author of *Dadland*

'. . . a beautiful book about love and loss, fragility and chance, the
wide world and the near world, and landscape and art. It is full of
intense light and colour, extraordinary glimpses, moving insights
and subtle humour.' Richard Kerridge, author of *Cold Blood*

'Mortality, aesthetic beauty, deep time and loss are themes never far
from the surface in this exquisitely written book . . . *Among the
Summer Snows* is at once haunting... ...l...
beautiful.' Alex Roddi...

D1078939

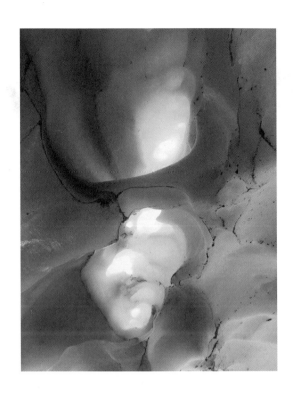

Among the

SUMMER
SNOWS

Christopher Nicholson

1 3 5 7 9 10 8 6 4 2

This paperback edition published 2018
First published in 2017 by September Publishing

Copyright © Christopher Nicholson 2017

The right of Christopher Nicholson to be identified as the author of this work has been
asserted by him in accordance with the Copyright Designs and Patents Act 1988.

Photography by Christopher Nicholson

On page 121, 'Gladly will I sell . . .' by Matsuo Bashō is from
The Narrow Road to the Deep North and Other Travel Sketches, trans. Nobuyuki Yuasa
(Penguin Classics, London, 1966), p. 60. Reproduced by permission of Penguin Books Ltd.

On page 123, 'My eerie memories . . .' by Hugh MacDiarmid is from the poem
'The Eemis Stane', in *Collected Poems of Hugh MacDiarmid* (Edinburgh & London, 1962).
With thanks to Carcanet Press for permission to reprint.

On page 137, 'What can the small violets tell us . . .' by William Carlos Williams is
from the poem 'Raleigh was Right', in *The Collected Poems, Volume II, 1939–1962*,
ed. Christopher MacGowan (London, 1988). With thanks to Carcanet Press
and New Directions Publishing for permission to reprint.

On pages 142–43, 'The Snow Party' by Derek Mahon is reproduced by kind permission
of the author and The Gallery Press, Loughcrew, Oldcastle, County Meath, Ireland,
from *New Collected Poems* by Derek Mahon (2011).

All rights reserved. No part of this publication may be reproduced, stored in
a retrieval system, or transmitted in any form or by any means, electronic,
mechanical, photocopying, recording or otherwise, without the
prior permission of the copyright holder

Book design by Friederike Huber

Printed in Poland on paper from responsibly managed, sustainable sources
by Hussar Books

ISBN 978-1-910463-85-7

September Publishing
www.septemberpublishing.org

To Hugh and Helen

I

IF THERE IS still a god, I sometimes think, he is not the great, crotchety being who was supposed to keep watch over us all. That ancient deity has fallen asleep or forgotten us, or he has become distracted by other concerns, or has lost patience with our pettiness, and instead we now have small gods, local gods, each with his or her specialist affiliation, a bit like a vicar with a parish. The river gods drip with mud and slime, the tree gods are long-limbed, spotted by mould, hairy with lichen, the desert gods are thin, shadowy creatures that move in the rippling hazes. The sea gods may be glimpsed like seals in bright water, their sleek, dark, bewhiskered heads appearing and disappearing in the troughs between waves some distance offshore. As for the gods of summer snow, I imagine them as short and muscular, trudging each late spring over the mountains to take up temporary residences in their allotted snowbeds. Deep in the ice, their features set in a disgruntled expression, they squat in silent, blue trances.

I first began to write about summer snow ten years ago. I had a plan for a book that opened in autumn, with the earliest falls on the Scottish mountains, and ended in summer with a walk to a great corrie in which the snow almost never melts entirely. The book went wrong when, a few months along the way, my wife Kitty fell ill. From then on, snow seemed much less important. For a while I tried to continue writing as if nothing had changed, but I could no longer justify the time away from home that walking in the mountains would involve. Besides, so much of what I felt about snow involved delight, and my main emotion now was one of deep foreboding. Before the summer was near its end, I gave up.

This short book, a decade later, is not about grief or consolation, at least not directly. It instead describes some walks to those last snows, the snows of late summer. That section of the old book, as I conceived it, was always the most interesting.

That there should still be any snow in Britain during the summer is strange. Summer is a season for easy living, a time of bees and foxgloves, roses and honeysuckle, light clothes and gentle breezes. Yet snow, a little snow, survives in the Highlands of Scotland. It does so not on the tops of the mountains, not like the bright white crown that sits on the head of Mount Fuji in Japan; this snow is much more obscure, hiding in isolated, difficult-to-get-to places under cliffs and crags, in clefts and corries away from the sun. Here the crystals gleam and glitter, shadow-bathing, hanging on to their essential selves. Some collections of snow are small caches of melting crystals, but others are as big as football pitches. It is their depth that really astounds. They can be as much as ten or twenty feet deep. Deeper, even. Higher.

Whenever I come upon one of these big snowbeds I do so with a degree of incredulity. That snow should still be here, so much snow, in the heat of the year, is enough for my mind to stand back amazed. The snow is counter-intuitive; its existence challenges the usual idea of what is possible. Then the amazement begins to give way to something less easy to define, a complication of thoughts and feelings.

Within this complication, among much else – curiosity, admiration, melancholy, elation – is uncertainty. The uncertainty of summer snow is part of its attraction, without a doubt. If I merely wanted to look at snow, any snow, if there was nothing more to it than that, I could go to the Alps. It's the lateness of the snow, the rareness of the snow, the improbability of the snow, that draw me up to the Highlands. The idea alone puts me on edge. Will any snow still be there? What will it be like? How big, how small?

I also know that walking to summer snow, especially in the early part of any walk, is good for thinking. Something about the business of walking, of gaining height, of negotiating uneven ground, something about the rhythm of walking, opens up my mind in an unusual way. This doesn't happen on an ordinary mountain walk, not to the same degree; the fact of the snow is critical. Perhaps, again, it is a matter of edge, but I think that I think better. I think about snow, but I also think about other things, and I even find myself thinking about thinking. When I reach some snow, if I reach some snow, I have an extra surge of mental energy. After leaving it, on the latter part of the walk when I am more tired, my thoughts tend to be old ones that I've run through before. Later, when I've recovered, I start thinking again about what I've seen and felt. A long period follows, in which all this beds down into memory.

One afternoon a few Octobers ago, a friend happened to ring with news of snow falling in the Cairngorms; there had been a report and photo in the Aberdeen-based daily, the *Press and Journal.* The first snow of the year. I was by the seaside in Kent, and as I browsed along the beach the sky was blue, the air soft and balmy, the light so sharp that every pebble was picked out in perfect focus. A herring gull – lemon legs, quizzical eye and blood on its beak – jeered over the decaying carcase of a porpoise, while the Channel waves turned and broke with the consistency of cream.

A forecast suggested that there might be more snow over the next week. On a whim I drove up; stayed the night in the Borders, and then drove on. From Perth northwards, I found myself scanning the dark, whale-like bodies of the mountains ahead. At last, as I came past the village of Kingussie and looked beyond the golden birches that lined the road, I sighted a paler mountain, draped in a cobweb. Since it was a good ten miles away, and since a cloud, also pale, hung on the shoulder of the mountain, the web might have been part of the cloud, or even a hallucination; but as the view expanded to include other mountains, I knew it could only be snow. A long road took me far above the treeline. A shower drifted towards me, and snow began to fall in little polystyrene-like beads that melted on the warm glass of the windscreen, and scurried over the tarmac. The clouds, low and heavy, lifted to open a gap through which a red sun shone, slanting a light that gilded a distant drape. It was late in the afternoon, and when the sun sank and the light grew grey, the snow seemed to float above the darkening land.

First showers like these are the opening passages in a long account. As the autumn advances there are further falls on the mountains, some light and tentative, others longer and more determined. Much of this early snow melts, but then the wind shifts to the north-east and winter closes its jaws. Now the snowfalls are heavier and more frequent. The snow spreads itself over the mountains, filling troughs and hollows, submerging rocks and boulders. Nothing melts in the cold air; the burns are frozen hard, even the cliffs are encrusted with ice. Around the new year the weather turns damp and soggy, and a small thaw begins to set in, but by now the snow is so well entrenched that it holds its ground. A few days later there is an immense blizzard. In late January and early February more storms follow, and the snow grows ever deeper until some point – maybe March, maybe April – when a southerly wind asserts itself. Then comes the big melt, and suddenly the mountains are no longer white but piebald. A final storm brings more snow, but after that a larger and more comprehensive thaw takes place. If you were to watch the disappearance of the snow over the Highlands accelerated into a matter of hours, on a speeded-up film, it would be like seeing lights dimming and going out on a dark night. By midsummer there are hundreds of pieces of snow left, but by late summer only a few are still shining. These are the last snows, the survivors.

❄

In preparation for the trip I spread out my maps of the Highlands and marked black crosses on all the places where I hoped there would be snow. Around Ben Nevis and in the Cairngorms, those were the two main areas. Some snow might lie further north, above Glen Affric, some further south, near Glen Coe, but there would be no snow near the west coast this late in the year.

I intended to stay in Scotland for all of August, but I wanted to keep things flexible. One warm evening I met an old friend. He hasn't been to the Highlands for many years, and nor is he that keen to go. What attracts him aren't quiet mountains but hot landscapes, simmering with fertility and colour. My interest in late snow has puzzled him for a long time.

'A month?'

'Yes. Unless I change my mind.'

He leant forward. 'Why might you change your mind?'

'I might . . . I don't know. It may rain all month. I may get bored.'

'But what is it? What's the attraction?'

'There are lots of reasons. The snow is often very beautiful, in an odd kind of way. And it's surprising. It's surprising that it's there at all, but it's surprising in other ways too. It's never quite what you expect.'

He eyed me. I could see his point: there are, on the face of it, more likely things to be interested in than summer snow.

'When I first went to Venice,' I said, 'I was slightly disappointed. I was disappointed because it was perfect. It perfectly matched the image of Venice in my mind. Nothing surprised me. But summer snow always surprises me.'

'But you've been there before. You must know what it looks like by now.'

'Not really. I know but I don't know. It's always different. Every year is different. And I feel different things about the snow every time.'

'Okay,' he said.

There was a pause. I felt a little defensive. 'I don't know exactly why I'm interested,' I said. 'I am because I am. If I did know, maybe that would be the end of it. Why are you interested in hot places? Because you went on holidays to the Med as a child. I went on holidays to Scotland.'

'So it's nostalgia? That's it?'

'No, I don't think it's that. In childhood things get laid down in the brain, that's all I mean. I was bowled over by Scotland when I was a small boy.'

'What if you get up there and the snow's melted?' he asked.

'If there's no snow at all? Anywhere? That would be interesting, too, in a way. But there's almost always some snow, at least in August. One snow almost never melts. In the whole of the twentieth century it only melted three times.'

This was my trump card, and he seemed moderately impressed. Then said, in a wistful tone: 'When I lived near Brighton I had a girlfriend who said that the pieces of dirty old snow by the motorway were like bits of her past that she'd rather not have.'

I was disconcerted by this remark. He was talking about roadside slush, filthy stuff, nothing like the snow in the Scottish mountains.

I pointed out that I wasn't alone in liking summer snow. In recent years, more and more people in the Highlands had become interested. Admittedly, the numbers were still quite small, but I wasn't a lone eccentric.

What I didn't tell him was how concerned I was about my physical fitness; that, not boredom or bad weather, was why I thought I might end up coming back before August was out. It wasn't so much my age, although I'd just turned sixty, a birthday that no one views with any great enthusiasm, but that ten months earlier I'd had an operation on my lower back. At a follow-up meeting with the surgeon, I'd asked if it would be okay for me to carry a rucksack in the summer. Well, he said cheerfully, it should be. But then he qualified himself. Not too heavy a rucksack. A light rucksack should be fine. Not too much weight. I see, I said.

As if a creaky back wasn't enough to cope with, I also had a dodgy left foot, a chronic problem under the bones of my second and third toes. This foot had been going on for years, and it had been X-rayed and ultrasounded and prodded and manipulated any number of times. Once there was a definite diagnosis, then a different diagnosis, then no diagnosis at all. Perhaps nerve damage, perhaps a neuroma, perhaps a bursa. It had become a mystery.

I went again to the lower limb consultant and he gave it a steroid injection. 'We may as well try. If it works you should be able to tell in a week or so. Where are you walking?' I mentioned the Highlands, whereupon he gave me a lovely professional smile and wished me luck. I couldn't interpret his smile, but I didn't think it reflected any confidence in the efficacy of the injection.

A week later, and the foot felt just as it had done before. Hot and bothersome. Maybe, I told myself, I would be able to walk off any pain, as one walks off a tight muscle; or maybe I should walk only on alternate days, giving the foot a chance to recover. The notion that it might be best not to go up to the Highlands at all did cross my mind, but I rejected it. I was sixty, and if I didn't go now, when would I? I had no intention of being beaten by a rogue foot.

My son confronted me as I was sorting through gloves and anoraks.

'How's your little finger?'

With some wariness I looked down at my hands. 'Fine. Why?'

'Everything else about you seems to be packing up, so I thought I'd check,' he said.

England in early August — the woods dark green, the wheat light gold, red admirals feeding on blackberry flowers, marbled whites drifting over the meadows. The swifts that nest every year in the church up the lane had just departed, one of the climactic moments of summer. They were travelling south; I drove north. There was a great deal of news on the radio. The latest on the US presidential election, the implications of Brexit, the threat of ISIS, fighting in Syria, terrorism in France. Dear God. The world's woes.

On a stop at a motorway service station, I drank my coffee and absorbed the scene. As if running counter to the news narrative, there was a sensible, matter-of-fact air to it all. People checking mobile phones, people standing in queues. Families on holiday, wearing shorts, T-shirts, sunglasses, baseball caps. A man in a shiny suit sucking the end of a pen, a woman in a blue tracksuit pedalling an exercise bike in aid of charity. 'Seriously summer' read the sticker on the plate glass window. Outside, Britain's post-industrial economy was on the move. Among so many thousands of people using the motorway that day, I was probably the only one with snow in mind.

It's true: there are many more likely, more obviously important things in which to be interested. Yet summer snow has preoccupied me for years and years. I've wondered if it may be a little to do with the business of writing. The pale screen of my laptop, or the white of paper, as a sheet of snow on which I make certain marks. In idle moments, I've even found myself typing an asterisk that reconfigures itself as a snowflake . . .

Still, I don't really think that writing explains much. More probably, it began when I was six years old and living in a pebble-dashed house on the outer edge of south London. Even then, as a little boy, I felt a constraint in the suburban environment, a sense of life hemmed by fences, roads, traffic, lawns and hedges. That Boxing Day snow came as a liberation. I loved the way it stacked as neatly on the tops of gateposts and walls and fences as if it had been edged by a ruler, and I loved the alternate creaks and crunches when I walked on it and the seething shiver when I pushed against the privet hedge in our front garden, and the flop of sound that a piece of snow made when it fell from a rooftop. I loved the silence, how silent our road was, although I could hear the sharp scraping noises of a shovel as one of our neighbours cleared his driveway, and I loved the arrow-like indentations left by birds' feet and the bent branches of the trees and the smoothness of things. My sister Clare and I could no longer tell where the road ended and the pavement began, and so we walked on the road, and if a car did appear it was only creeping along, we could easily get out of the way. We swept a space in the yard and put out crusts for the birds, and filled a Fray Bentos pie tin with warm water so that they had something to drink. Within a couple of hours it had iced up. We knocked out the ice and filled the tin again. When more snow fell, the flakes descending in mazy lines, we ran round trying to catch them in our mouths, and later we snowballed Bacchus. He was a rescue mongrel with black fur and brown eyebrows and a white shirt-front, and we loved him. We used to sit in the bath, chanting 'Who's the best dog in the world, who's the best dog in the world? B – A – C – C – H – U – S, the best dog in the world!'

That long, snowy winter is my first memory of what might be described as a public event. The Cuban Missile Crisis of

October 1962, two months earlier, when the world blinked and recoiled at the prospect of nuclear war, has left no trace, and nor do I have any recollection of the assassination of President Kennedy in November 1963, but I can remember that when we went tobogganing Clare and I wore knitted balaclava hats and that Clare's balaclava was red and mine blue, and I can remember that my anorak was dark blue while her anorak was creamy-white with a flower pattern, and I can remember how my wellington boots filled up with slush and how terribly cold my feet were as I plodded home in the fading light with the snow orange under the street lamps. The snow lasted for nearly three months, and there were days when the roads were blocked and we missed school. Then it ended, and the world returned to its normal, tight, unromantic self, but I was left with a permanent blaze of white in my memories.

Was that how it began, or was it Scotland? Scotland was my other country. Not every year but most years in my childhood we drove up there for our summer holidays, visiting my aunt and uncle, who lived on the coast north of Aberdeen, and borrowing their caravan to explore the Highlands. The country was the antithesis of suburbia, the quintessence of wildness. It had lochs, pine forests and mountains. Its wildlife included eagles, wild cats, pine martens and otters. Secretly, I felt as much Scottish as English.

This wasn't only a matter of romantic sentiment; some hard facts backed me up, or at least what I thought of as facts. My surname was Scottish, there was a proper Nicholson clan, and when my parents went Scottish dancing on winter evenings at the local Caledonian Club, my mother wore a long pleated skirt in the Nicholson tartan, the cloth chequered green and blue. She was entirely English, but my father was Scottish. That is, he had been brought up in England, he had the most

English of accents and he had never lived in Scotland, but his parents and grandparents had been Scottish and he was therefore Scottish by blood.

Blood was critical, I felt. My blood was half Scottish, half English: if it were analysed, would my mixed ancestry show up in two separate streams?

At times I was a little confused. When Scotland played England at rugby or football, it was hard to know which side to support, and things became difficult when, at the age of seven, I was sent to a nearby school for boys run by an eccentric Scottish headmaster who wore a kilt and tweed jacket, and had a bone-handled dirk in his thick woollen socks. He was a ferocious old man with a neck like a bulldog. To my astonishment, he insisted that in the winter terms any boy with a Scottish association should also wear a kilt. 'But I don't want to,' I told my father, 'I can't wear a kilt! I can't!' A kilt was a skirt, it felt sissy; in my panic I was ready to renounce any links to Scotland. My father told me that lots of other boys would be wearing kilts and that I would soon get used to it. I never did. After all, this wasn't Scotland, it was south London, and if, having collected me from school, my mother had to go to the shops, I would stay in the car, hiding my bare legs from public view.

Almost no Scottish history was taught at the school. I learnt that 1314 was the date of the Battle of Bannockburn, someone told me about Robert the Bruce and the spider, and I vaguely imbibed the tale of Bonnie Prince Charlie's flight after the Battle of Culloden in 1746, but I had no idea what lay behind any of it. Even if I had known more, would it have made any difference? I was so infatuated with the idea of Scotland that I tried to speak with a light Scottish accent, chanting place-names to myself. Killiecrankie. Crianlarich.

Tulloch. Loch. 'Lochhh.' 'Mo-o-o-r-r.' 'Bur-r-r-n.' Burns seemed better than streams. In my mind they connected to fire, liquid fire, tumbling down the mountains. When I was grown up, I decided, I would definitely live in Scotland, in the Highlands. For years I believed that when we went to Scotland, on those summer holidays, we went uphill.

It would be handy if I could conjure a specific childhood memory – a hot day in the mountains when I was eight or nine, and saw a snowbed at a certain distance, and ran towards it and fell upon it. A photograph of Clare and me posing by the snow would be even better, confirming those holidays as the origin of my interest in summer snow. But in those pre-digital days people took many fewer photos than they do now, my father probably had only enough film for twenty-four exposures each holiday, and there is no snow in the albums. Did we find it on our walks? I think we did, but where, and was it once or several times? And, if so, why don't I remember it more clearly? Why, instead, do I merely have a glimmering sense of that old snow?

In my mid-teens our family holidays ended, but I continued to come up to the Highlands by myself. At sixteen, equipped with a second-hand copy of Keats' poems, wearing a pair of inadequate felt boots and carrying my father's old rucksack, a thing of heavy canvas with narrow leather shoulder straps that gouged the thin flesh on my collarbones, I spent three weeks tramping the mountains. When I was twenty-two I and a university friend walked from the west coast to the east; by now I had a better rucksack, but wore heavy boots with metal shanks. I clumped along. Not only do I remember the blisters, but I still have their scars on the backs of my heels.

When I was twenty-six I came here with a new girlfriend. Like me, Kitty had been brought up in London suburbia, and she was also intensely romantic about wild landscapes. She introduced me to the paintings of Caspar David Friedrich, I introduced her to the Highlands. We caught the night sleeper from King's Cross to Fort William and woke as the train was crossing the great expanse of Rannoch Moor. Bog, cotton grass, thin birch scrub, pools of dark water. Not the usual scenery in which to fall in love, maybe. After we married, we continued to come up to Scotland; after we had children, we came up as a family. After she died, I came up with my son and daughter and we buried her ashes on the top of Quinag, her favourite mountain, far in the north-west, from which the views reach to the sea and achieve a blueness more blue than any other I know.

I thought about some of this as I drove along the motorway. How places come to acquire deep personal meaning. But I also thought that if I had lived all my life in the Highlands I might have well been driving in the opposite direction, heading south in search of green fields, lanes lined with cow parsley, footpaths linking old churches and quiet pubs. I wouldn't have been on the hunt for summer snow.

❄

After crossing the border I took a detour. Some miles west of Gretna Green lies the village of Mouswald where my Nicholson ancestors lived a few generations back. I went to the church, a striking whitewashed building with a slate roof and a little tower, prominently placed high on a bluff above pastures in which brown and black cattle were grazing. It was a bright day with low cloud, and a breeze that rustled the leaves of the beech tree near the church. Some white gulls meandered by, and the air smelt faintly of salt. In the distance, light shone on the waters of the Solway Firth. I had never been here before.

In the churchyard stood more than a hundred upright tombstones, reddish in colour, all facing away from the direction of the westerly wind and rain. Sandstone is noted for its durability, and the inscriptions, running back to the eighteenth century, were as sharp as if they'd been cut a few years ago. By a clipped yew bush I found a large stone, some seven feet high, a memorial to Jonah Nicholson, farmer, of Howthat. Jonah Nicholson was my great-great-great-great-grandfather; born in 1747, he died in 1833 at the age of eighty-six. His wife, Ann Carruthers, is the next name on the stone, dying three years before him at the age of eighty-four.

What was their life like? An account of Mouswald in the 1790s, given by the minister, the Reverend Mr Jacob Dickson, paints a picture of a quiet agricultural parish. The farmers grow oats, barley and potatoes. The population is six hundred and twenty-eight. There are forty-eight farmers, sixty cottagers, two millers, ten day-labourers, one hundred and forty-two horses, seven hundred and fifty-three black cattle, three hundred and eighty-six sheep. 'Everyone keeps a pig.' 'Each marriage, at an average, produces 5 or 6 children.' 'No account is kept of children dying under 2 years of age,' he writes, presumably because infant mortality was so common. It felt good to see that below Jonah and Ann's names on the memorial was that of their first child, John, who died after just thirteen days.

The memorial was very possibly erected by Christopher Nicholson, their fourth son, who became the vicar of Whithorn. I was named after him. It is often said that memorials honour the dead, as if that was all that needed to be said, but there is something to add about the use of stone as a medium. Stone is among the most enduring of materials. Inscribing the names of the departed in hard stone so that they can still be read generations later is an implicit assertion that the dead are worth remembering, that their lives were worth living, even if they lived only for a few days. The same is true of writing in general. To notice something enough to write about it is, at the least, a tacit acknowledgement of its value.

Howthat was half a mile from the churchyard. Not even a hamlet, it was a modern farmhouse with some older outbuildings, and a sign on a wooden fence that warned of guard dogs. So this was where my four-times-great-grandfather, to whom I owed the fact of my existence, had lived. I had a suspicion that while he might have been pleased at my visit to the graveyard, he would not have begun to comprehend my attraction to summer snow. Other things surely occupied his mind: the cutting of hay, the condition of his animals, the business of putting food in the mouths of his family. In all likelihood, if there had been summer snow in the low hills near Mouswald, he wouldn't even have noticed. I may be wrong. He lived long before the age of mass refrigeration, and it's possible that the sight of snow in August would have intrigued him.

Driving on towards Glasgow, I was aware of a niggling anxiety. Was I going up at quite the right time?

Deciding when to visit the Highlands is tricky. If you go in midsummer there is always plenty of snow on offer, and this is a good time to see specialist birds like dotterel and snow bunting, which breed high on the mountains. Yet there are good arguments for going later, for as the snows melt they become more curious. They develop characters, although even as I write that I feel a qualm: how can a piece of snow possess character? But their individuality becomes more distinct with the advance of time. They show signs of their age. They sag and ripple and crack, and exhibit new and intriguing features – tunnels, arches, bridges. And, day by day, their survival grows more and more precarious.

Should I have been making this journey earlier, in mid-July? Or earlier still? The amount of snow left in late summer depends upon the amount of snow that falls in the preceding months, and then upon the speed of melting, as determined by the weather. Sun, rain, wind. All highly variable.

The previous year, I knew, had been freakish. A cool spring had been followed by such a cool summer that there had been repeated falls of snow on the mountain tops. No less than eight days in June had been snowy, and a prodigious quantity of snow had survived deep into August. This year seemed much more average.

In May I'd made a flying visit to the Highlands, and as the aeroplane crossed the Cairngorms I peered from the porthole and saw snow beneath me. I drove up to Ben Wyvis, the hulking mountain north of Inverness. Robins and willow warblers were singing furiously in the woods at the foot of the mountain. Young conifers pushed out spurts of brilliant green growth, bracken unfurled muscular fronds. The air was warm and friendly. Yet, on climbing the Ben's steep shoulder, I found myself in a cold fog. Ben Wyvis isn't a mountain that I know well, and I walked along to the summit cairn. There I ate my sandwiches and wondered where any snow might be. A cyclist – I'd overtaken him on the climb – pedalled up and we had one of those laconic, downbeat conversations that often seem to take place in casual encounters on the mountains. Would the fog lift, probably not, sod's law. But the fog was thinning even as we spoke, and I suddenly made out the light of something brighter. Two shallow snowbeds lay in dips of ground, like bunkers on a golf course. Then larger slabs of snow materialised along the mountain's steep southern flanks, a procession of pale ghosts. The sun burst through and a magical transformation took place: the snow shone, the stones glittered with fragments

of mica, and from some far-off vale there floated a cuckoo's faint call: cuckoo, cuckoo, cuckoo.

The sound of early summer. Since then, the weather up north had been generally mild and cloudy. It wasn't easy to know how things would be, but only a little snow might have survived. I shied away from the possibility that there might be none at all.

2

HUMID AIR, LOW CLOUD and biting midges: welcome to the Highlands. In the carpark below the Cairngorm plateau, people were flapping their arms and running for cover. For a moment or two I sat in the car, reluctant to leave its safe space and face the world; then I flung open the door and tore out. I pulled on a hat and anorak, took off my shoes, slotted my orthotic insoles into my boots, put on thick socks, put my feet in my boots, tied the laces, stuffed my rucksack with overtrousers, gloves, a banana, some sandwiches, a bar of chocolate and a water bottle, checked that the compass and whistle were also in the rucksack, remembered my camera and binoculars, tightened the straps of the rucksack and slung it on my back. By now the midges had found me, they were biting my neck and face and hands, they were on my eyelids and in my ears. I slammed shut the car boot and, adjusting my walking poles, set off at the briskest pace I could muster. Ahead there was a slow walker around whose head the midges were apparelled in a fuzzy turban. When I caught her up and muttered a greeting, she said: 'Ah, the midges are cruel today!'

My intention was to climb to the plateau via the fork that leads into Coire an t-Sneachda, the corrie of the snows, *coire* or *choire* being a mountain hollow and *sneachda* one of many similar-sounding descendants from the Indo-European *sneighwh* or *snoigwh* or *snigwh*; among its close relatives are the German *schnee*, the Gaelic Scots *sneachd* and the Irish *snechta*. The first written record of this sn- word in Anglo-Saxon dates from around 825, when it was spelt *snauw*, and it seems clear that this was how people pronounced it. Then there was a change, which probably came about through the influence of Norman French: somewhere around the twelfth century, the word 'snow' starts to appear in written records instead of *snaw*. The Gloucestershire village of Snowshill, listed in the eleventh-century Domesday Book as 'Snawesille', has become 'Snoweshull' by the year 1251. But it was a while before the spelling standardised, and some experimentation took place; in the late fourteenth century, William Langland wrote of a dunghill that was 'bysnewed with snow'.

As I climbed the path, I caught a glimpse of white on the cliffs of the adjacent corrie, Coire an Lochain. So I changed my plan and went up the shoulder of the corrie. Dark cloud sat on the top of the plateau and the upper part of the cliffs, and although I thought I'd seen the white of snow, I wasn't sure. I stopped and waited. The cloud fumbled over the cliffs in a dreamy fashion, while from the jumble of rocks below there rose the strange, creaking calls of a ptarmigan. I could remember the day when I'd stood near here and watched a male ptarmigan engaged in the art of courtship. He was grouse-like, but with fluffy white underparts and white tufted legs, and a head topped by a vermilion crest. The hen, a bird of fabulous quiet beauty, was so well camouflaged that she was hard to see until she moved. Her grey plumage was a mass of dots and speckles, with a faintly greenish tinge towards the neck and head, matching the colour of the lichens on the rocks. She tilted an eye towards the cock, who took off on a low flight in which he soared about thirty feet in the air, swept back, landed on a boulder near the hen and gave a little waggle of his tail. How about that? he seemed to be asking. She pecked the ground, whether in appreciation or dismay I couldn't tell.

The cloud continued to sidle over the cliffs of Coire an Lochain, and after a while I gave up and walked on. Soon I was on the plateau, a great plain of rock and bog. Four thousand feet above sea level, it must be one of the most exposed areas in Britain. The wind pours and drives across the land unobstructed by trees and boulders, and there are only a few dips and hollows that offer shelter.

Now it was a fog-bound sauna, the air eerily still. Droplets of moisture grew on the lenses of my glasses. Wearing glasses is a definite disadvantage when walking in rain or fog or drizzle, especially if you're as short-sighted as I am. Take the glasses off and everything is a disconcerting blur, keep them on and a screen of moisture intervenes between your eyes and the rest of the world. As I walked along, I could see the blurry green patches of alpine lady's-mantle, the occasional lump of white quartz, some pinkish-grey rocks covered in dark lichens. I passed a cairn and noticed a quick movement. What was that? To my amazement, a vole, dark brown, shot towards my feet. Only for a second; the next, as if yanked by an elastic band, it had disappeared under the stones. What an inhospitable place to find a creature like a vole! Surely life would be easier at a lower altitude?

After half an hour of rapid walking, I followed the path

down to a saddle of land. On the saddle there is a little lochan, Lochan Buidhe, with *buidhe* meaning yellow or gold. Now, in the fog, the water was dull blue. Shallow, dead still, very quiet. A black beetle swam away.

I dried the lenses of my glasses and walked round the lochan. Then saw a glimmer of light on rising ground. Ah, ah. Hurried towards it; then stopped hurrying. There it is, you fool, it won't go away; take it easy.

Walked up more slowly. The snow lay in some wrinkles of land, and I did what I always do, came to the first bed and pressed a palm on its cold surface, as if to assure myself that the information given by my eyes was correct. Yes, it's snow, it really is! Summer snow! None of the snowbeds was very large, but the mere sight of them was lovely. They were surrounded by dark, scoured, gravelly ground. Long scarves of bright water ran downhill from their bodies.

Had I been here a month earlier, there would have been much more snow. That was clear enough, but I wasn't complaining. I took off my rucksack and circled the snowbeds, fascinated by their shapes. From a certain angle one reminded me faintly of a long fish. It had a dark eye and a tail. Another was a thin white shadow.

The largest snowbed didn't remind me of anything. It didn't have a regular shape and it lacked any symmetry. Near it, a fragment of snow was wrapped round a dark rock blotched with black moss and lichen. Two crystal arms curved downwards, hugging the rock and triggering an association that I couldn't quite put my finger on. Bones decorated with pearls? A holy relic? A heraldic shield?

Another snowbed lay half a mile away at a spot called Coire Domhain. *Domhain* means 'deep', but the fold of land that comprises the corrie isn't that deep, and the pitch of this snowbed wasn't steep. It was big, though. Thirty or forty yards long and twenty yards wide, it had spread itself over the uneven ground in a rough fan shape. Some reindeer were grazing nearby, and although two or three raised their heads and watched with soulful eyes, the others paid me no attention as I picked round the snow. It was melting fast from below, but it was still intact, a single solid body.

Certain features intrigued me. I noticed what, if the snow had been deeper, would have become a tunnel. I noticed a particular hole in the crystals, a perfect circle, and puzzled as to why it was there. My eyes moved between the darkness of the hole and the whiteness of the crystals. I noticed, on the pale surface of the snowbed, a single reddish gold leaf on which the veining was still visible. It was probably a bilberry leaf, but there on the snow it looked like a piece of burnished metal on display in the window of a jewellery shop.

I wondered whether to walk over the snowbed. Some people have no compunction about walking on summer snow, but I always have this odd feeling: am I showing a lack of respect? Does the snow mind? Then I tell myself that this is snow, only snow, how can snow mind? Don't be ridiculous. So, despite my reservations, I shin up and walk on the snow. I pass two clutches of ptarmigan or grouse droppings; around each one the snow has melted in a neat ring. Near the centre of the snowbed lies a blackish object that might be a rock but turns out to be, unmistakeably – I prod it with the end of my walking pole – a deer turd.

That was all the snow I saw in my first day in the Highlands. A few possible pieces of snow on the cliffs of Coire an Lochain, some interesting relics near Lochan Buidhe, and a big snowbed at Coire Domhain. Not a lot, but enough to whet my appetite; and as I walked off the plateau I felt suddenly more confident

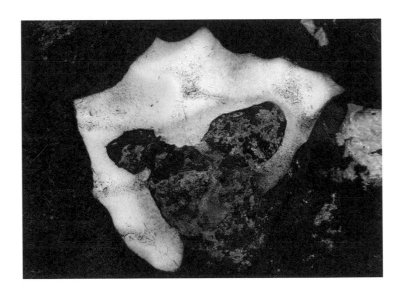

about the month ahead. I had doubted whether, in my ropey state of health, I would be able to cope with the physical challenge, but four or five hours of lugging a rucksack round the mountains didn't seem to have adversely affected my back, and my left foot wasn't troubling me too much. Of course, this had been an easy walk, and there were tougher ones to come, but so far so good.

Early the next morning I drove back to the Cairngorm carpark. With high cloud and blue sky the midges were no longer biting. I wanted to check that I hadn't been mistaken about the snow at Coire an Lochain, and I took the same path as before. Now the cliffs were clear and sunlit, and the specks of snow visible from a long way off.

Snow at all seasons is wonderfully reflective – brighter than

water, brighter than the faces of wet rocks – but late summer snow, high on the side of a dark mountain, has a particular, eye-catching quality. None of the pieces of snow here on the cliffs of Coire an Lochain was much bigger than a shoebox, but they stood out brightly. They lay in two inaccessible areas, one to the side of a bulge of gnarled rock known as the Great Slab. Years ago, two winter climbers were knocked off the Great Slab by an avalanche that carried them into the lochan below with such force that they were buried under ice. The bodies were recovered only in the spring. The sun now had still not reached the lochan, and it was dark as a grave. The other pieces of snow were a hundred yards further to the west.

Once on the plateau I cut across boggy ground to the north of Ben Macdui, Britain's second highest mountain. This is a reliable place for late snows; even in a hot summer they generally survive on the steep cliffs above Loch Avon. I arrived at the edge of the cliffs to see the loch stretching away for nearly three miles, a blue mirror cradled by sweeps of pink and grey scree.

Below me, on a flattish ledge of rock, lay the first snowbed. Waist-deep, it was a frozen swimming pool. Its gleaming surface was covered with bits of plant debris, mostly broken stems and stalks.

We generally imagine snow as pure, and the notion extends itself into the moral sphere: so snow is chaste and innocent. Virgin snow. 'She was pure as snow, then she drifted . . .' goes a joke that supposedly originated at Yale University in the 1920s. But only new snow is pure; old snow, snow that has survived from winter into summer, is dirty. And yet this is lovely dirt. Leaves ripped from stems of bracken, sprigs of heather, tips of club moss, the wings of a beetle, lie in sheets of illuminated crystal. Sometimes this matter is thinly spread, but on occasion you find withered scraps of grass in such quantities that they stand up like the stumpy bristles on a worn-down broom. The surface of the snow can be as hairy as the flanks of a donkey. When the composer John Cage saw the 1951 *White Paintings* by Robert Rauschenberg he memorably described them as 'landing strips . . . airports for lights, shadows and particles'. Summer snowbeds are exactly like that, blank spaces on to which stuff happens to have dropped.

Curiously, however, the debris never looks haphazard. Invariably, there are hints of aesthetic intention in the way that the material lies, inducing the sense that a minimalist artist has been secretly at work, decorating the snow to make it more interesting and beautiful. The debris here was delicately patterned, as if someone had drawn on the ice with a stick of charcoal.

A hundred and fifty feet further down the cliff there was an even bigger snowbed, a monster. I knew that it was special the

moment I set eyes on it, but working my way down the cliff, over ledges of wet rock and moss, took a good ten minutes. After much tracking to and fro, I was on its level.

Snowbeds usually turn out to be larger than they seem at a distance, and this was some eighty yards across and thirty yards wide. At its edges it was at least ten feet deep. What made it so thrilling was the sense of rapid and powerful movement that it seemed to embody. While the first snowbed had communicated immobility and stasis, this angled into the cliff as if it had crashed at speed. Into my mind there came the image of a bird of prey in full flight, a peregrine slicing through the air.

A stream ran under the snow and issued from its lowest point. Here I crouched and looked up a short tunnel with glistening walls. It vanished into the darkness. A waft of chill air, the snow's outbreath, met the skin on my face.

Several blocks of snow, once part of the main body, now detached, lay on the same level. One had a snow bridge and I

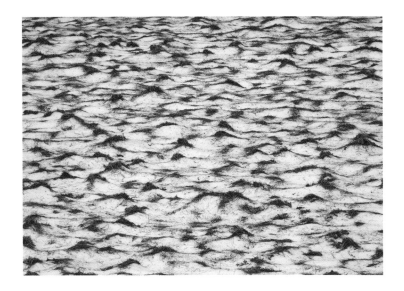

stood underneath it. The icy underside of the arch was as smooth as polished marble, and its colour was a faint, spectral blue.

I love this blue. It's something you often see when looking into snowbeds; it's there in icy cracks and tunnels and holes. What I mean by spectral is that the blueness feels less than stable. The colour flows and slides over the white of the ice in an indeterminate fashion. Photos of snow tend to exaggerate this blueness, which makes me wonder which blue is the right blue. Are my eyes correct, or is the camera? Is either correct?

The front edge of the arch was scalloped in a series of uneven curves, and on the lowest part of each curve water gathered and built to a glassy drop that bulged and fell. As I watched this building and falling and building again, with the light in each swelling drop, I noticed an insect, a crane fly with six long, spindly legs, flying repeatedly into the ice. No doubt it was attracted and confused by the glare of the crystals.

It settled, folding its gauzy wings. Light shining through the crystals shone through the wings.

At moments like these it's hard working out where to focus. My gaze shifted to another growing drop of water. If I moved my head, I could look through the drop to the waters of Loch Avon, far below.

Beyond the bridge there was another isolated hunk of snow, and this was so arresting that I found myself walking towards it very slowly. It leant to one side and had the appearance of a ship beached at low tide, or cast up by a great storm. Here it was in its final resting place on the cliffs of Ben Macdui, among the hard rocks, abandoned by its crew. The flat upper deck was covered in untidy debris, while the keel was smooth and white.

I circled it for a while, a bit dazed and spellbound, like the crane fly; then wrenched myself away. Contoured further along the wet cliffs, cut up the side of the mountain. Set off a hare, which stood on a ridge, ears erect, perfectly silhouetted, before making off in a low crouch of a run. Some time after this I realised that I had lost my hat, had probably left it by the snow bridge. To make it even worse, it wasn't really my hat but my daughter's. It was a woolly hat with a complicated zigzaggy pattern of blues and reds, and I hadn't even told her that I'd borrowed it. I would have gone back but my legs were tired, and I decided to leave it for another day.

❄

I was staying in a small cottage near Kingussie, not far from the Ruthven Barracks, where the defeated remnants of the Jacobite army gathered after the rout at Culloden. I strolled there in the late afternoon. Still largely intact, the stone fortress stands above

a vast expanse of marshy, grassy ground now managed as a bird reserve. A solitary red deer browsed in a watery ditch, a heron took off from some reeds and flapped for a few slow yards. Rabbits were feeding on a low gorsey hill in the middle of the marsh, and presently a hen harrier got up and turned in the air above the rabbits, which seemed oblivious of any danger. These quiet goings-on were curious to set against the Barracks where, more than two and a half centuries earlier, the Jacobite soldiers impatiently waited for the arrival of Bonnie Prince Charlie. He never came, instead sending instructions that they should return to their homes, and so the rebellion came to its end.

I was watching the harrier – it pounced, but missed – when the puzzling snow fragment that I'd seen near Lochan Buidhe came back into my mind. Of course! The famous Viking helmet that archaeologists discovered in a grave at Sutton Hoo, with its long earpieces curving under the chin – that's what it was like! At some time I must have seen the helmet in a glass case at the British Museum, and now my brain had matched it with another image, that of a few snow crystals. And it wasn't as if I'd been consciously thinking about it. In some deep area of my mind, a fizz of secret electrical activity must have been taking place.

When, having returned to the cottage, I clicked on an internet image of the helmet and compared it to the photo of the crystals, I was a little deflated. Far from confirming my insight, the helmet wasn't very like the snow. That is, it was and wasn't. There was a strong resemblance all right, but the helmet was the helmet, the snow was the snow. I ran through some of the other analogies that I'd contemplated: a fish, a swimming pool, a bird of prey, a wrecked ship. A ship! Hmm. Had that snow really looked like a ship?

Describing individual summer snows is a challenge.

Complex and untidy, they arrange themselves not in squares and rectangles and circles, but in irregular shapes that come from the land on which they rest. Hence the recourse to analogy: like this, like that. Isn't that cloud like a camel? Hamlet asks Polonius. Polonius: 'By the mass, and 'tis like a camel, indeed.' Hamlet: 'Methinks it is like a weasel.' Polonius: 'It is backed like a weasel.' Hamlet: 'Or like a whale.' Polonius: 'Very like a whale.' While Shakespeare is certainly pointing up Polonius' obsequiousness, he is also suggesting the futility of trying to trap clouds in a net of words.

Since the age of Shakespeare, much energy has been devoted towards the ordering of the natural world. We now have a system to differentiate different cloud types − stratus, cumulus, stratocumulus, nimbus. We have words to distinguish different sorts of birds − red grouse, ptarmigan, twite, raven, golden eagle − and different forms of water − loch, lochan, river, burn, stream. These words are shorthand, every loch and every river is different, but they are useful. No system of classification exists for Scotland's summer snows, however. Nor would it be easy to devise one. The late snows commonly lie on slopes that face between north and east, and at a height of 3,500 feet or above, but there are no obvious types.

Even finding the right generic term is hard. 'Snow-patch', which is now in widespread use, tends to give a false impression. If I ask people who've never been to northern Scotland what it brings to mind, they describe small, shallow areas of snow left in shady field corners. No, I say to them, truly, it's nothing like that! Think deep! Think mountain icebergs!

Over the years I've toyed with alternatives. 'Snow-field': no, too contained, too organised, implying fences, hedges, gates, and anyway it tends to mean an area of permanent snow. How about 'snowdrift'? The term comes from the Old Norse − 'drift'

from 'drive', therefore 'driven snow' or 'driving snow' – and has two meanings. In its first, it describes snow that is literally being driven through the air. In its second, it refers to a piece of snow that, having been driven, has accumulated in ditches and hollows, or against walls and hedges, and in this sense a 'drift' is a (relatively) settled, solid object. I like 'drift'. I also like the beautiful word 'wreath', which has slipped a little out of use, though in north-east Scotland it is still current. 'Wreath' links to 'writhe', and is sometimes particularly used to describe a curved drift. In Scotland, there are three mountains – Ben More, Cairn Gorm and Lochnagar – with wreaths known in Gaelic as the *cuidhe crom* – the crooked wreath. The problem with both 'wreath' and 'drift' is that they are wintery words. They belong in another season.

That's why, in the end, I plump for 'snowbed'. It's not entirely satisfactory, since beds tend to be soft and horizontal, while summer snow is hard and usually lies at a steep pitch.

But these seem minor objections when set against the implicit thought of the snow quietly asleep in a bed of its own making. Dreaming through the summer months. Alive.

Thinking of the snowbeds as alive or partly alive is more than a piece of fancy. True, they are not alive in the way that a tree or a fish or an insect is alive – they are not capable of reproduction, for instance – yet they regulate their own internal temperature and adjust to external stimuli. They are also biographical phenomena, with pasts and presents and futures. In their first existence they were part of the sky, drifting, airborne – in the second they're on earth, solid and icebound – and in the third they become water, running to the sea. Above all, it is their sheer presence that suggests life. This is something that I occasionally feel in medieval churches. Especially when the churches are small and quiet, when there's no one else around, the air seems full of a knowledge that runs back for centuries. The stone walls, the dark pews, the altar, are waiting and listening. And there is that powerful feeling that if I too were only to wait and listen, if I were only to wait long enough and listen hard enough, then something of significance might happen, although it is difficult to put a finger on what that something might be.

Snowbeds have a similar power, which explains why I am reluctant to walk on them. It is as if to do so might be sacrilegious. But perhaps all I am saying is that, whatever they may be on the ground, they come alive in my own mind.

The night after visiting Ben Macdui I had a dream in which I saw a roundabout of snow. It was a perfect tablet, bright white, and cars were slowly circling it, nose to tail, in silence. There was something a little funereal in the image but it didn't develop, and whether it had anything to do with anything I've no idea, but it indicated the extent to which I was being infiltrated by snow. The snow wasn't only in my upper consciousness, it was drifting lower.

3

WHEN I RETURNED to the snowbeds I failed to find the lost hat. It wasn't by the snow bridge; either someone had picked it up or I had dropped it elsewhere. The fog was back, thicker than before, which didn't help. As I worked round the cliffs of Ben Macdui I was cautious and apprehensive, aware of the hidden drops and the slipperiness of the rocks. The snowbeds manifested themselves as amorphous glares. They were huge lightboxes. Their white bodies merged with the white tissues of the fog.

Snow is famously white; the idea besotted sixteenth-century English writers. Edmund Spenser's *The Faerie Queene* mentions 'snowy lockes', 'a snowy Palfrey', 'a snowy Swan', a 'snow-white smocke', 'a beard as white as snow' and contains no less than seven approving references to 'snowy breasts'. 'Fairer than whitest snow on Scythian hills' is how Christopher Marlowe describes one of the characters in *Tamburlaine*, while Shakespeare has Juliet declare that Romeo 'wilt lie upon the wings of

night / Whiter than new snow on a raven's back'. Since the time of Aristotle there had been interest in what it was that made snow so white, and now in 1563 William Fulke attempted to explain the whiteness: 'Snowe is whyght, not of the proper colour, but by receiving the lyghte into it, in so many small partes; as in fome [i.e. foam] or the whyght of an egge beaten.'

The foam and eggs are wrong, but Fulke was not far off. The whiteness of snow is caused by the internal properties of the crystals and the way in which they evenly reflect all the light frequencies. Yet the quality of the white varies greatly. Under a moon the whiteness acquires a steely note, under sun it has a golden sheen. There is a different sort of hue at dusk, when the ability of snow to radiate light seems most remarkable. In a summer's twilight, in the gloaming – a word that has the same root as 'gloom' but also links to 'glow' – snow gives the impression of gathering light to itself. It opens its arms and embraces the light. This phenomenon, known as the Purkinje shift, is in truth

nothing to do with the snow, but results from the adjustment of rods and cones within the human eye to changing light conditions. It occurs not only at dusk, but also in fog.

Fog and snow stand in a strange and sombre relation to each other. Both are versions of white and both are made of water, but you don't experience the two phenomena as discrete. The white of the snow is perceived through the white of the fog, the white of the fog is affected by the white of the snow. As an observer you are implicated: you look through the fog, you breathe in the fog. At times it feels as if the fog is seeping into your head, filling the cavities of the mind.

There on Ben Macdui, the power of what I couldn't see but could only imagine was considerable. As the snowbeds stretched away, disappearing into shades of white, I was struck by their immobility: unlike the fog particles, which danced before my eyes, they were utterly still. The longer I looked at them, the brighter they became. I thought that if I could burrow into their depths I might find their energy centres, pulsing waves of luminosity. If the world had been plunged into total darkness, the snowbeds up here would still glimmer away.

A Christian legend describes summer snow in fourth-century Rome. An elderly couple, wealthy but childless, wanted to know how to dispose of their property in a way that would honour God. They prayed to the Virgin Mary, and on 5 August 353, a surprisingly precise date, they had a dream in which the Virgin appeared. Where snow falls, she said, build a church. When the old man and his wife awoke, they learnt that snow had fallen on the Esquiline Hill. Here they built a basilica, Santa Maria Maggiore, that stands to this day as one of Rome's great churches; among its relics is a casket containing a piece of wood supposed to have come from the manger in which the infant Jesus lay. The miracle of the snow is commemorated every 5 August with a scattering of white petals from the dome of the church on to the altar. The legend was first recorded in the early medieval period, when veneration of the Virgin was growing, and in the fifteenth and sixteenth centuries it became a popular subject for Italian artists. Among them was Masolino da Panicale, whose painting, from about 1430, is a highly stylised affair featuring a yellow sky occupied by a fleet of disc-shaped clouds. According to some UFO enthusiasts, these clouds are alien spacecraft. With Jesus and the Virgin watching from on high, and a crowd of nuns and priests in attendance, the red-robed Pope Liberius uses a mattock to cut the holy snow into the shape of the church's foundations. The snow is emblematic of spiritual light. A friend of mine, a poet, visited Santa Maria Maggiore and wrote a poem that imagines the immaculate snow falling out of the darkness: 'lighting the starred night with itself'.

❅

Light opposes heaviness as well as darkness, and in this respect the big summer snowbeds are not light. They are hulks of ponderous, dense matter that bear down upon the land, and their weight, if they could be weighed, would be colossal. They are also hard. Anyone who wanted to dig deep into a snowbed would need a pickaxe. Yet — and the thought never seems far away — the millions upon millions of crystals that form the snowbed were once soft and airy. They were specks of almost nothing, almost as light as light itself.

A snow crystal begins its life high in the doughball of a cloud, when a molecule of water vapour freezes on a particle of dust or sea salt. The molecules forming the baby crystal are arranged in a hexagonal lattice, in which atoms of hydrogen and oxygen — two oxygen to every one of hydrogen — are bonded along horizontal and vertical axes. The crystal grows rapidly, sprouting plumes and pillars and spurs and spikes, and eventually it becomes heavy enough for gravity to take hold. Pulled and dragged on the currents of the wind, it sinks towards the ground. The wind is critical in determining what happens during the descent. Sometimes, and this is often the case over the Scottish mountains, the ferocity and strength of the wind smash the crystals into fragments; but other falls are calmer and quieter and the crystals remain intact. They sweep gracefully into land with a swirl that hints at the turn of a ballroom dress, or they flutter like petals, or rock like feathers. In Lincolnshire a traditional saying was that 'the old lady is shaking her feather pillows out of her window', in Gloucestershire people would remark that old Mother Hawkins was plucking her geese, and in Oxfordshire the rhyme went: 'There's the old woman a-picking her geese, An' sellin' the feathers a penny apiece'. A nice variant comes from the Lake District, where in the late eighteenth century the young Wordsworth was told that 'they

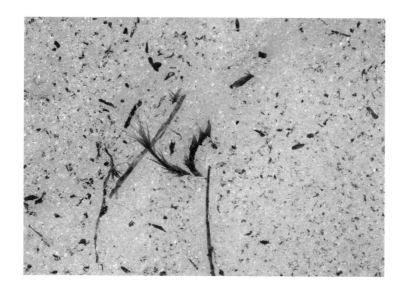

are killing geese in Scotland and sending the feathers to England'. These feathery flakes are the ones that I seem to remember from my suburban childhood, big, complicated agglomerations of crystal drifting slowly through the orange of the night sky.

Such flakes are intensely vulnerable. Tread on freshly fallen snow, and it gives with a satisfying crunch, or 'crump' – the onomatopoeic word used by John Clare. That sound is the snapping of so many delicate spokes and the expulsion of trapped air under the weight of the foot. But as the snow packs down, as the last air is squeezed out, there is less crumping and crunching, and if the snow survives long enough – if it deepens, and forms what might be described as a snowbed – an extraordinary transformation takes place. Snow is not unlike a metal in the way that it's able to change its physical structure, undergoing a process known as sublimation in which a substance changes from a gas to a solid, or a solid to a gas, without passing through the liquid state. Within the hidden depths of the snowbed, water molecules evaporate as vapour from the tips of one crystal and reform on another crystal as ice. Once so fragile and idiosyncratic, the crystals are remade into a body of similarly shaped, rounded, tightly knit grains.

This process feels like a survival mechanism, and fits with the sense of the snow as alive. Put a hand on it, dig in your fingernails, scrape up some crystals. How unscientific but how tempting to think of the snow collectively remaking itself as an act of will, hardening its inner core and outer shell, a creature strengthening its defences in a hostile world.

4

THE WEATHER TURNED back to sunshine, and I drove to Creag Meagaidh, which rises unobtrusively above Loch Laggan in the central Highlands. As I put on my boots, a middle-aged woman climbed from a dark blue sports car. 'Are you going up the Window?' The Window is the pass that leads to the summit ridge. I said that I was, though I was really interested in snow – and I showed her my map, with its crosses to mark possible snowbeds. 'Oh,' she said, 'last July I came up here with my son, and when we passed some snow he said, "I'll stay here, you can go on," so I left him there to play in the snow.' When I asked how old her son was, she replied that he was nineteen. 'Well, nineteen last year, twenty now. But you're never too old.'

The path climbed through a lovely stretch of mixed woodland. Dappled shade. Birches, rowans with clusters of orange berries, patches of dark green bracken. Willow warblers calling, that signature song, like the fall of bright water. A pale brown moth feeding on a pinky-purple flowerhead of devil's-bit scabious. Then I was beyond the wood and in an area of more scattered birches, the lichens on their trunks and boughs giving them a hoary appearance. The Creag Meagaidh estate is nowadays a National Nature Reserve and deer are culled to encourage the spread of new trees up the sides of the mountains. The sloping ground between the birches was purple with flowering heather.

As the path curved round the north side of the valley, the massive cliffs of Coire Ardair came into view. High on them two snowy shapes were shining. One was near the top of the ridge, the other in a thin gully that fell many hundreds of feet to Lochan an Choire. Among the fish in this small loch are Arctic char, or charr. Charr are cold-water fish, and after the melting of the Ice Age glaciers more than ten thousand years ago, some populations of charr were left isolated in individual lochs. Here, unable to escape and breed with other populations, they have become genetically distinct, and scientists say that the charr in some lochs now look very different to the charr in other lochs. There are even single lochs in which live two or more genetically separate strains of charr. I have never seen a charr except in films, where they appear as graceful, dark grey fish, with orange-red underbellies and white-edged lower fins.

After passing the loch I reached a point from which I could see the gully more clearly. This is Raeburn's Gully, named after a pioneering Scottish mountaineer of the late nineteenth and early twentieth centuries. The gully was dark and narrow, with the snow wedged into a rocky cleft. It had a mottled appearance like the back of a lizard, and it was also a bit lizard-like in shape. Below it lay a long and steep chute of scree. The scree looked very loose and I decided against climbing the gully. Easier to descend to the snow from the ridge.

Went on, up the Window. At the top of the pass there was

a strong warm wind, with a long view west over pale bog to distant mountains. Another walker came down the side of Carn Liath and joined me. He was hot and puffing. He lived in Stirling, had driven up for the day; was collecting Munros, had been doing it for three years. His partner had been hoping to join him but she couldn't get off work. 'It keeps happening,' he said, 'she gets jealous of me.'

I asked him how many Munros he'd climbed. 'Seventy so far.' Then he said, a little apologetically: 'Well, it's a good excuse to see the scenery.'

'Did you happen to see any snow on Carn Liath?'

He was surprised. 'Now? No.'

On my map I'd put a cross on Carn Liath, some way east of the summit. 'Sometimes it has a little late snow. Last summer it had snow.'

'Not now. Not that I saw.'

From his rucksack he unpacked a large supermarket baguette.

One in the afternoon and I climbed up to the plateau, a flatland of pale yellow grasses. Prints of deer in patches of dark mud. Mountain sorrel, alpine lady's-mantle, alpine club moss. A cloud shadow hung over a faraway lochan, giving it a metallic sheen.

The absence of snow on Carn Liath didn't surprise me. What was the temperature now? Twenty-five degrees, perhaps; more in the sun. Snow was an endangered species.

I walked along the top of the cliffs and edged down a grassy bank towards the Raeburn's Gully snow. It wasn't easy to reach, the slope was steep and I now thought – too late – that after all I would have been better to have climbed up the gully. Here I was, however. I got down on my knees and crawled as far as I dared. The snow looked even more like a mottled lizard,

skulking quietly, trying to keep out of the sun's direct glare.

After tracking back, I walked towards the other snowbed. Much more exposed than the lizard snow, it hung below the ridge in a broad scoop of rocks and crags. Under the high sun its white crust was glossy as wet paint, and across this crust jagged a blueish shadow, the edges so sharp they might have been cut by scissors, like the profile of a series of Alpine peaks. The snow seemed settled and secure, but when I scrutinised it through binoculars I noticed two cracks in the side of its body. I began to wonder whether, instead of gradually shrinking, there might be a moment of sudden catastrophe when the snowbed lost its grip and crashed downhill.

Climbing down to the snow tempted me, but the slope was precipitous, and whichever route I took would have involved a twenty-foot descent over gleaming black rocks. I had no ropes, and my ice axe was back in the car. Had I been younger, had I not been the sixty years I wished I wasn't, I might have risked those few feet, but you get more cautious with age. Why is that? Possibly because in the course of those years you've seen and heard of too many things that have gone wrong, or because the less time that you have left the more you cling to it, or because you are more aware of the consequences of tragedy for those you love.

Anyway, no big deal. I lounged on the ridge, eating my lunch, gazing at the white of the snow and the blue of the sky, and the views of Loch Laggan and its sandy shoreline.

❄

One of the first writers to take note of summer snow was an Englishman called Edmund Burt. From the late 1720s to the mid-1730s he lived in Inverness, where he worked as a government engineer. He may well have been involved in the construction of roads and bridges in the Highlands. Possibly out of boredom more than any idea of publication, he wrote a long series of letters to a friend in London, and in one such letter he turned to the matter of the local landscape.

> The Highlands are, for the greatest part, composed of hills, as it were, piled one upon another, till the complication rises and swells to mountains, of which the heads are frequently above the clouds, and near the summit have vast hollows filled up with snow, which, on the north side, continues all the year long.

In what follows, he does not attempt to conceal his profound dislike of the scenery. The colour of the mountains he characterises as 'a dismal gloomy brown drawing upon a dirty purple'. Their rugged and irregular ridges are 'rude and offensive', while the panoramic views are 'most horrid' – 'for then the eye penetrates far among them, and sees more particularly their stupendous bulk, vast irregularity, and horrid gloom'. Yet, despite his general antipathy, the existence of summer snow clearly challenges him. One June day he goes to investigate, and steers his horse over a snowbed: 'the surface was smooth, not slippery, and so hard my horse's feet made little or no impression on it; and in one place I rode over a bridge of snow hollowed into a kind of arch'.

Burt is a very good writer, well aware of the difficulties of describing natural forms – 'Language, you know, can only communicate ideas, as it were, by retail . . . from words we can only receive a notion of such unknown objects as bear some resemblance with others we have seen . . .' – and one phrase that he uses is very apt: 'the spaces of snow near the tops of the mountains'. It catches something of the imprecision of the snows and their tenuous hold on existence. If the snow did not exist, there would be a space; as it is, the snow does exist, not only occupying but also becoming the space.

A few decades later, in the late summer of 1773, James Boswell and Dr Samuel Johnson famously undertook a long journey through Scotland. They were, on the face of it, an unlikely pair of companions to find in the mountains. Boswell was thirty-two years old, a bright Edinburgh lawyer who loved city life, while the sixty-three-year-old Dr Johnson – whose travelling outfit involved a brown suit, a large wig, worsted stockings, boots and a greatcoat with pockets almost big enough to accommodate the two volumes of his *Dictionary* – was in poor health. He was overweight, and according to one biographer his ailments included 'lumbago, muscular inflammation of the loins and belly, and a bronchial inflammation'. He also nurtured a deep-seated prejudice against Scotland, and it was only after

Boswell's intervention that he left behind a pair of pistols and a supply of gunpowder and bullets. Instead, as if to emphasise the strength of his feelings, he armed himself with a large stick of English oak. This staff mattered to Johnson. It was a symbol of all that he represented – common sense, sturdiness, civilisation – on his foray into the north.

Travelling west of Inverness, they stopped at a wayside inn in Glen Moriston for the night. It was not a happy experience. Both men were worried about bedbugs (Boswell could not get to sleep for fear that a spider might drop into his open mouth) and also secretly concerned that their landlord might murder them in their sleep. Riding on, the next morning – it was 1 September – into a wild country that, by repute, was almost as threatening as Afghanistan today, they were still jittery. Memories of the 1745–46 Jacobite rebellion remained alive – their landlord, who walked a little way with them, had fought at Culloden – and so frayed were their nerves that, as they entered Glen Shiel, they proceeded to have an argument about terminology. Boswell, who thought that the peaks flanking the glen were 'prodigious mountains', referred to one as 'immense', which earned him a tart rebuke from the great lexicographer: 'No; it is no more than a considerable protuberance.'

Both later published accounts of their trip, and it is Boswell who, poker-faced, relates this hilarious exchange. Dr Johnson, in a regal description of the day, merely alludes to it by forcibly restating his position: 'Of the hills, which our journey offered to the view on either side, we did not take the height, nor did we see any that astonished us with their loftiness.' He goes on, however:

Towards the summit of one, there was a white spot, which I should have called a naked rock, but the guides, who had better eyes, and were well acquainted with the phenomena of the country, declared it to be snow. It had already lasted to the end of August, and was likely to maintain its contest with the sun, till it should be reinforced by winter.

These iron-clad sentences are marked by a scrupulousness of language, and also a certain distaste. 'A naked rock' is not a phrase that suggests any approval on Dr Johnson's part, and the word 'reinforced' implies that military matters remained on his mind. As for Boswell, he does not even mention the snow in his account of the journey, presumably deciding that it was of insufficient interest.

If, one early September nowadays, you were to trace Boswell and Johnson's route down Glen Shiel, you might or might not be impressed by the protuberances on either side of the road, but you would be most unlikely to see any snow. Experts disagree on the precise duration of the Little Ice Age, but the term is generally used to describe the period from about 1300 to 1850, with temperatures dipping to their lowest points in the seventeenth and eighteenth centuries. In Britain the winters were often long and savage. Snow is thought to have lain in southern England for a hundred and two days in the winter of 1657–58, and for sixty days in the winter of 1683–84. In the Scottish Highlands, it snowed for thirteen consecutive days in the winter of 1620, and there were months and months of snow in seven out of the eight winters between 1693 and 1700. One estimate puts the snow line at three to four hundred metres below its present level.

Snow went hand in hand with cold, and few people viewed it with anything but antipathy. One shouldn't be surprised that neither Boswell nor Johnson was impressed. Yet the fact that their local guides bothered to point out the white spot is significant. They were aware of the new fashion for wild scenery, and thought the snow might be of interest to the two gentlemen. As it turned out, it wasn't; but there were a good few eighteenth-century travellers, especially in northern England and north Wales, who raised an eyebrow at the sight of summer snow and found themselves speculating as to how long it might last. Daniel Defoe, writing in the late 1720s, mentioned snow on the top of Snowdon in the month of June, but went on to say that 'it does not continue the year round, as some have asserted'. Cross Fell, in the Pennines, was similar – Bishop Richard Pococke noted snow lying on its middle and northern slopes 'towards July' in 1760, and there is another record from 18 June 1785 – but William Hutchinson, in 1794, firmly stated that 'snow has never laid a whole year upon it, within the last seventy years, as I have been assured by the shepherds'.

In 1787, James Clarke published a tourist guide to the Lake District, in which he describes how Helvellyn 'rises with precipice over precipice, and hides his rugged summit amidst almost continual mists. Snow is seldom a wanting here . . .' He then gives over the page to an account by a gentleman who had climbed the mountain specifically for the snow.

I had often, from the neighbourhood of Penrith, seen specks of snow in the height of summer, on the summit of a hill, the name of which I did not at that time know; and a strong desire seized me of dining in so elevated a situation, and upon such a seat as is not at all common in Britain at that season. Accordingly, about two o'clock of a midsummer morning, I set forward, and rode about eleven miles to Glencoyn, which lyes at the bottom of that heap of mountains on the summit of which this snow was seen. Leaving my horse at the house which stands in this small valley, I began to ascend: it was now betwixt four and five o'clock, and I experienced what I would not have believed possible at that time in the morning, viz, a heat greater than I have felt in any situation at noon ... with severe toil I, in about five hours, reached the snow, and the summit. The surface of it was covered with dust, so that I was obliged to make a hole in it with my staff to procure clean snow to drink, or rather eat to my dinner ...

Ah, this gentleman, this early snow pilgrim, my kindred spirit: how much I would like to meet you. If time were able to reshuffle itself, if it might arrange a midway rendezvous between then and now, I would try a few questions. How old were you when you climbed Helvellyn that distant summer's day? Were you a local, living near Penrith, or were you one of the new wave of mountain tourists? What lay behind your strong desire (that word 'seized'. . .), and what did your friends and family think of your exploit? In hindsight, was the snow worth the effort?

A little may be inferred. He was a gentleman, and therefore a man of some means, with enough leisure to eye some distant specks of snow, and then to think about them. He was energetic enough to ride in the dead of night from Penrith to Helvellyn, a considerable undertaking – the road taking him along the shore of Ullswater to Glencoyne Farm – and to climb the mountain as dawn broke. He was confident enough to write down an account of his adventure, and, presumably, to consent to its publication.

Clarke's judgement that the exploit was 'curious and

singular' is a useful reminder that climbing a mountain to look at some old snow was still a distinct eccentricity. Yet tastes in scenery were now changing fast. The elderly Thomas Bewick, who lived much of his life in the snowy north-east of England, remembered that in the 1780s 'to be placed in the midst of a Wood in the night, in whirlwinds of snow, while the tempest howled above my head, was sublimity itself', and there is equal enthusiasm, if of a quieter kind, in Dorothy Wordsworth's journal entry from Grasmere for 12 December 1801:

> A fine frosty morning – snow upon the ground . . . We played at cards – sate up late. The moon shone upon the water below Silver-how, and above it hung, combining with Silver how on one side, a Bowl-shaped moon the curve downwards; the white fields, glittering Roof of Thomas Ashburner's house, the dark yew tree, the white fields – gay and beautiful. Wm. lay with his curtains open that he might see it.

In April 1805, a romantically minded young man set off with his dog on another solitary ascent of Helvellyn. His name was Charles Gough. More than three months later a shepherd found his dismembered remains and scattered clothes beneath Striding Edge, one of the rocky ridges that leads to the summit. Striding Edge isn't difficult for ordinary walkers to negotiate in good weather, but becomes a trickier proposition in ice, and Gough may well have slipped. Remarkably, the dog was still with his body, still alive – its barks had attracted the attention of the shepherd – and had even given birth to a puppy.

Gough was a jobbing landscape artist, and his demise in the wilds of Helvellyn fitted the myth of the solitary romantic in search of sublime experience. The loyalty of the dog made the story even more attractive, and among those to hear of it was Wordsworth. In 1805 he had already written two poetic tributes to dogs, and this tale, from a mountain that he knew so well, was a gift. Yet in setting the scene for 'Fidelity' he introduced a detail absent from the newspaper reports:

> It was a cove, a huge recess,
> That keeps, till June, December's snow;
> A lofty precipice in front,
> A silent tarn below!
> Far in the bosom of Helvellyn . . .

This is more than incidental. 'Bosom' is a word that Wordsworth uses elsewhere around this time when he is describing something that lies near the heart of spiritual experience, and 'recess' also hints at the secret and holy. 'The close recesses of my soul,' wrote Alexander Pope in *The Iliad*. Wordsworth's poem offers Gough a peaceful end among the snow in one of nature's churches. A stone memorial, quoting from Wordsworth, was erected on the broad summit of Helvellyn in 1890, and stands to this day, its face beautifully patterned by pale green lichens.

As I sat above the snowbed on Creag Meagaidh two ravens flew nearby, their wings stroking the quiet air. One landed by an outcrop of rock and, after a little rearrangement of its plumage, tilted its head in my direction. Ravens are intelligent, curious birds and I had the strong impression that it was thinking about me. I thought about it. Its dark plumage had a purple sheen. I could see the feathery tufts on its slate-grey bill.

After a moment, it stepped to the edge of the rock, leant forward and tipped itself into an easy flight that took it away, past sunlit crags.

One of the hard-headed ideas advanced to explain the mysterious condition of Gough's remains on Helvellyn was that his corpse had been attacked by ravens. Another blamed the dog – how else could it have survived so long without starving? Wordsworth's romantic version wasn't the only one on offer, and there were people who criticised Gough for his folly in attempting the mountain without a guide. While this is unfair – Gough in fact employed a guide who then withdrew at the last moment – the sense of a certain rashness remains. He was just twenty-one, a risk-taking age, and a man who met him before the fatal expedition described him as 'venturesome'. In the light of his fate, I felt my decision not to climb down to the snowbed was the right one; a little slip on those rocks might be all it would take. Yet I felt a measure of disappointment at my prudence. So near, and so far. It would have been better if I could have touched the snow.

On 4 July 1816 another gentleman – or, just possibly, the same one as in the 1780s – climbed Helvellyn in pursuit of summer snow. He collected a lump and brought it down to the office of the local newspaper, the *Kendal Chronicle*. 'The gentleman informs us that he saw three or four patches of snow, varying in extent in different directions,' the newspaper reported. Kendal is even further from Helvellyn than Penrith, and it's nice to picture the moment when he triumphantly exhibited his icy trophy in the newspaper offices. Here it is – proof! Feel it! Again, there are religious undertones: this is an early nineteenth-century version of the scene in which the resurrected Jesus upbraids Thomas, the doubting disciple: 'reach hither thy hand, and thrust it into my side: and be not faithless, but believing.'

I can understand the gentleman's pride. Summer snow is a miracle, a piece of out-of-season magic: to see it is one thing, to make physical contact with it is another. Queen Victoria's Highland diaries note how, on 18 August 1860, climbing Lochnagar, she 'scrambled on to where there was a great patch of frozen snow, just below the top of the hill. Sat there a moment . . .' Touching the snow, licking it, eating it, clambering over it, sitting on it, are ways of engaging with the sheer surprise that attends its existence. I've collected snow myself, more than a few times, although once it has been removed from its surroundings and put in a freezer it looks much like any other lump of ice.

A more recent example of snow collecting comes from the summer of 1963, when snow lingered long above 2,000 feet on the Cheviots. By late June, five pieces of snow were still visible in gullies above the Bizzle Corrie on the hill's north face, while beside College Burn, above Hen Hole, there was a big snowbed that survived at least another month. One Billy Gilbert had a bet with his uncle that he couldn't produce snow at Kelso Show on the last Saturday in July, and he went up into Hen Hole and got some in a flask.

Driving away from Creag Meagaidh that sunny afternoon, I stopped to pick up a couple of hitch-hikers with heavy backpacks. They were students in their early twenties. Joss was German and came from a small village outside Bonn; Helga, his girlfriend, was Austrian and lived in Vienna, although she too had been brought up in the countryside. They were heading for Inverness Airport after six weeks of walking in the Highlands, camping and staying in bothies. They'd had a great time, although once with night falling they'd misread the map and lost their way.

'The mountains are so big,' said Helga, 'if you make a mistake and go down the wrong valley, it's difficult. And it was getting dark. We found the bothy in the end, but it was worrying!'

They laughed at the memory. After that we talked about the differences between walking in the Alps and walking in Scotland. Joss and Helga said they preferred Scotland because it was so much wilder, so much closer to nature, although the midges were bad.

'When people told us about the midges, before, we thought we would be able to, you know, clap our hands and kill them . . . we didn't know they would be so tiny! And so many of them! The first night, when we were camping, it was incredible!'

I told them that smoking a pipe was meant to repel midges – that was what my father had done on our long-ago caravanning holidays in Scotland.

'Yes,' said Joss, who was sitting with my ice axe in the back of the car, 'and I smoked many many cigarettes, but in the end you can't smoke all the time. Helga doesn't smoke.'

Helga said: 'Still, they did not attack me as much as Joss.'

They asked me what I was doing in Scotland and I explained that I was up here to look at the remains of the winter snow. Both of them understood immediately.

'Ah yes, good, that's great,' Helga said enthusiastically. She had better English than Joss. 'Both of us, we love snow. So there is still snow here?'

'A little. Not a lot, not like in the Alps. Just in a few places, scattered here and there . . . you haven't seen any on your walks?'

'No. Have we? I don't think we have.' She appealed to Joss.

'Have we seen snow?'

'No,' he said.

'We haven't been on the tops of the mountains very much . . . you know, with packs, you know . . . But there is still snow, that is good.'

The road wound on and our conversation shifted to Britain's vote in favour of leaving the European Union. I was interested to know what they felt, and it turned out that they were sorry but not surprised. A few weeks earlier Austria had had a presidential election in which a far right-wing nationalist had nearly been elected, and the election had then been annulled as a result of irregularities in voting. There would be a rerun later in the year, and Helga was very worried that this time the nationalist would win.

'It would not be good for the country. It would be bad.'

'But isn't it a ceremonial role?' I asked. 'How much executive power does an Austrian president have? How much real power?'

'Not so much, no, it is limited,' she answered, 'but I am still frightened. There are ways to change things. Hofer, if he is president, he may be able to make the country much more right-wing. It's not the young people in Vienna who vote for him, it's the people in the countryside, that's the problem. Old people in the countryside. They don't like foreigners, the immigrants, they don't like Europe.'

'It is the same in Germany,' Joss said.

'But you come from the countryside, you were brought up there.'

'I do, ja. Ja.' I could hear the shrug in his voice. 'But everyone in my home village is very right-wing, all are. We are very divided.'

'We are divided here in Britain too,' I said, although I could see that the spectre of right-wing nationalism would be particularly alarming in Austria and Germany.

I asked Helga and Joss if they felt the root cause lay in immigration, or whether there might be something much larger at work to account for the rise of popular nationalism. After all, it seemed to be happening in country after country. Was it about unemployment? Or was it a reaction to the pace of globalisation, to the way the internet threatened the sense of local identity? They responded politely: yes, it was all that as well.

They were an engaging couple with their lives ahead of them. Once they had finished their respective courses – Helga was studying drama, Joss mechanical engineering – they planned to live together in Vienna. I hadn't intended to drive as far as Inverness, but I thought I could usefully do some shopping. When I dropped them off in the city centre I wished them luck; they thanked me, put their packs on their backs, and walked towards the hostel where they were planning to spend the night. I drove to the supermarket.

5

SUNDAY MORNING. Light breeze, blue sky, high cirrus tissues in slow motion, as if caught in some gentle current. 'Cirrus' comes from the Latin for 'curl' or 'wisp', which brings hair to mind, but these long, trailing, bending fibres, maybe thirty-thousand feet above the earth, were composed of ice droplets shining in the sun. I was on my way to one of the best known of late summer snows: Ciste Mhearad, which translates from the Gaelic as Margaret's Coffin. It lies less than a mile from the summit of Cairn Gorm, and the snow has been known to reach a depth of as much as sixty-five feet. When every other scrap of snow has vanished from the ski slopes of the Cairngorms, determined skiers occasionally come here to enjoy themselves.

Visiting snow on a hot summer's day brings the business of temperature into sharp focus. As you climb – climbing is always involved – the actual air temperature decreases but your body temperature goes the other way. So you have to decide: do you take off one layer or keep it on? You keep it on, reasoning that although you're a little too hot you're still okay, but after another minute you're definitely overheating. Off comes the layer, but then the sun moves behind a cloud and the wind gets up and you're suddenly cold, and you put the layer back on. Then before you know it the sun is out again and this time you can't be bothered, it's too much effort to stop and take off your rucksack and fight the zip that always seems to stick, and so you go on, getting hotter and hotter, asking yourself why on earth you packed gloves and overtrousers – although you know why, because the weather up here in the mountains can turn quickly, it would be stupid to do anything else. Finally, in a state of febrile heat, you come upon the snow, which is an image of cool composure. As human beings we live on a narrow ledge, a few degrees in either direction and we're in deep trouble.

I was curious to see Ciste Mhearad not least because it was described in 1801 by Sarah Murray, an early writer of guidebooks for female travellers with a taste for romantic scenery. Aged fifty-seven, wealthy and upper class, she had come up to the Highlands from her home in London in order to collect material. On 7 September, after breakfast in Glenmore, she set off to ascend the mountain. She was accompanied by four gentlemen, who walked; she rode on a pony, which is one way to avoid overheating. Although there is no record of their conversation, it probably touched on the subject of earthquakes. That very morning, at six o'clock, an earthquake had struck Scotland; although its centre lay ninety miles to the south, the shock was strong enough to be felt in the Cairngorms.

In her account of the expedition, Murray recommended that readers should visit what she called 'the snow house':

The snow house is not far from the Cairn or heap of stones, on the highest part of Cairngorm, and is a hollow, in extent an acre or two. This hollow is filled with snow, and although it faces the south, it is never melted by either the sun or rain. Near its boundary, on the south side, runs a stream of the purest water; in its bed are large stones, standing high and thick, serving for supporters to the roof of snow, which seems to be in some degree petrified. There was little water in this stream that day I was at it, I therefore, by bending my body, walked up the bed of this rivulet for three or four yards, without getting very wet; but it was so intensely cold under snow and in water, that I was obliged quickly to return . . .

More than two hundred summers later, seen from the slope above, the snowbed did not look anything like a house. It was also smaller than it had been on Sarah Murray's visit, probably no more than half an acre. That said, it was an impressive island of ice. When I climbed down to one of its edges it rose to the height of my neck, but at the centre it must have been much deeper. Its surface was uneven, with trenches and hollows and corrugations, implying a well-advanced structure of unseen melt. At its upper end, two streams ran down the slope and, having joined, cut a tunnel through the snowbed. It was possible to see about ten feet down the tunnel. It tapered into a glow of ill-defined, blueish light that came from the sun above shining through a thin patch of crystals. At the other end of the snowbed the stream emerged, bubbling in its passage over rocks and gravel and cushions of black moss. I pictured Sarah Murray lifting her long skirts and bending her body in order to advance up the tunnel.

I also bent my body, but the tunnel was too narrow and the stream too full for me to go far. The uneven sparkle of the stream contrasted with the smooth sheen of the tunnel's ceiling. This ceiling was composed of similarly sized plates that curved and met in sharp ridges. Along the ridges ran thin dark lines as if to accentuate their particularity. Plates like this develop out of the passage of air across the slowly melting crystals.

I retreated, and spent a while examining a large section of ice that stood a few yards apart from the main body. It was long and curved, and on its side it had a stratified pattern of debris: that is, there were two layers of snow-ice, the lower much more thickly covered in debris than the upper. I was uncertain how to interpret this – no doubt a snow scientist would have seen the answer straightaway – but I knew that some snow here at Ciste Mhearad had survived from the previous summer. What now constituted this lower layer might have fallen from the sky a year and a half ago.

Depth is critical in the meaning of these snowbeds. As each fall adds another layer to the snow, the bed becomes a record of time past, time frozen. It resonates like Ted Hughes' pond: as deep as England. I think this is why the idea of tunnelling carries such appeal. Victorian explorers believed that only by travelling into the interior of Africa could they understand its mysteries, and scientists, whether investigating the earth or the human body, have always known that the most important truths lie not on the surface but deep within. To tunnel into or under a summer snowbed is to go back in time. I am envious of the Reverend William Forsyth, who one August day towards the end of the nineteenth century arrived at Ciste Mhearad to find the tunnel ten feet high and more than a hundred feet long, and was able to walk under the entire length of the snowbed.

*

The name of Ciste Mhearad, or Margaret's Coffin, was clearly not known to Sarah Murray, and must have been given to the snowbed in the nineteenth century. So who was Margaret? Folk tales were popular in the late Victorian and Edwardian years, and writers of the time offer two possibilities: first, that this spot in the mountains was long ago haunted by 'a wretched hag who had been driven from society for her crimes, and she herded goats and found a grave'; second, that Margaret was an incarnation of a famous Highland witch, the Witch of Moy. This story of this witch is given in 'The Curse of Moy', a long gothic poem by John Morritt that Sir Walter Scott inserted into Part Three of his *Minstrelsy of the Scottish Border*, published in 1802 and 1803. A mountain witch arrives at a banquet and reiterates an old curse on the first-born of the Clan Chattan, the Mackintoshes, whose ancestral seat is Moy Hall near Inverness. There is no mention of snow, however.

To confuse matters further, there is a second corrie in the Cairngorms named Ciste Mhearad. Lying some eight miles away above the heathery slopes of Glen Feshie, it too is a good gathering place for snow. It faces west, which leaves it vulnerable to rain, and by late summer the snow has usually melted, though in recent years it has survived as late as 3 September. A 1910 guidebook links this corrie with the Witch of Moy ('a certain Margaret, who had been jilted, died here in her mad wanderings, after having cursed the Moyhall Mackintoshes to sterility'). However, there is an alternative tale:

Long ago a Glen Feshie maiden loved a youth who for some crime was ordered to be hanged by the laird. She sought his life with tears, but her prayers were unheeded.

In her grief for the loss of her lover she committed suicide in this wild spot: the snow is her pall.

Well, good stories. I settled above the snow, on a slope of pink gravel and young green moss. Ate a sandwich and a nut bar. Thought of snow and death. How far back into Western culture the link runs. The pale horse of death, the dead covered by white shrouds, winding sheets, the coldness of death, the coldness of snow.

This is an association that everyone knows, but in different guises. In one, the snow is kind and gentle. So it appears in the diary of the Reverend Francis Kilvert in late December 1878, a time of deep snow in the Welsh borders, the roads icy and the River Wye freezing over. On Christmas Eve the snow is sparkling in the sun as Kilvert goes to comfort the parents of a young boy, Little Davie, who died on the previous day. Mrs Davies, his mother, takes Kilvert upstairs and turns down the sheet. 'I never saw death look so beautiful,' Kilvert writes that evening.

> The pretty innocent child face looked as peaceful and natural as if the child were asleep and the dark curls lay on the little pillow. I could hardly believe he was dead . . . Before I left the room I stooped and kissed the child's forehead, and the mother did the same. It was as cold and hard as marble.

Reading this, it's clear that Kilvert's feelings are informed by the presence of the snow outside, especially when Mrs Davies proceeds to tell him that before Little Davie died he had a vision in which his sister was pelting him with snow and ice. It seems appropriate that when, the next day – the afternoon of Christmas Day – Kilvert takes the funeral service, snow should be 'driving in blinding clouds', while the bell, the Welcome Home, 'chiming softly and slowly to greet the little pilgrim coming to his rest', sounds 'bleared and muffled through the snowy air'. As the burial takes place, snow falls on the coffin.

Snow is not always soft and reassuring. Snow is also violent and deceitful and unreliable, and over the years it has been the cause of many deaths. 'There are three smiles worse than sorrow,' runs a triad from ninth-century Ireland: 'The smile of the snow melting, the smile of your wife to you after another man has been with her, and the grin of a hound ready to leap.' Ciste Mhearad may well have acquired its name not because of any witches or hags, but for a simple reason: that a woman called Margaret died up here in a snow storm.

Nowhere is this treachery more blatant than in the case of avalanches. The commonest form of avalanche in Britain is known as a slab avalanche: what typically happens is that snow falls on a steep slope, settles, compacts and freezes. A second fall of snow follows, landing on top of the first. The two layers of snow do not merge but remain separate, and in a state of instability. At a critical point the instability resolves itself, with the top layer of the snowbed detaching itself and sliding down in a slab.

Ten years ago, when writing the book on snow that I never completed, I talked to Mollie Porter, who was once avalanched in the Cairngorms. We met at the Speyside Heather Centre, north of Aviemore. She got out of an ancient car and limped towards me, trying not to put any weight on a bad ankle. Ginger hair, face beautifully lined, eyes sparkling.

She wasn't Scottish. She'd been brought up in Hertfordshire, and had started her working career as a teacher in Birmingham. But what she lived for was climbing, and in the summer of 1960 she went on an expedition to an unexplored area of north-west Spitsbergen. There were six on the expedition, including Joe, her husband. Dropped off in Magdalena Fjord by a mail ship, they sledged hundreds of miles and climbed twenty-two previously unconquered mountains. At the end of the summer the boat collected them and brought them back to Tromsø. Soon after that, she and Joe came to the Cairngorms and began to work as winter climbing instructors. She became a member of the local Mountain Rescue team; for twelve years she was its leader. She became well-known for her common sense and courage in extreme weather.

'The Cairngorms in the summer,' she said, 'they can be beautiful, if you get right into the heart of the Cairngorms; but in the winter it's transformed into this sort of savage place, you know, and it's seriously difficult to handle. It's a real challenge. I mean the Cairngorms in winter are extremely dangerous. The weather up there can be appalling. I did a science project for seven years on the summit of Cairn Gorm and I've been on my hands and knees in a white-out. Have you ever been in a white-out?'

'I haven't.'

'Well, the worst is if you're on skis, because you don't even know you're moving. You see there's no light, no shadow . . . there's nothing to focus your eye on that gives you perspective. I've experienced it in Norway; we were in the Hardanger area, on a survival course, and we were cross-country skiing, and we all kept falling into hollows. Because you couldn't see they were there! There were no shadows! But a white-out in the Cairngorms is ten times worse because it's thick white! Everything's white! You're in this white soup and it's so dangerous. You've got to be very good on navigation and timing. The most dangerous situation is when you're coming off the plateau, because you're coming north to a cliff edge, and the cliff edge in winter will have a great big cornice hanging over the edge of the cliff, and to be on the edge of the cornice is too far. The fracture line for a cornice is way back from the cliff edge. So you're coming at right angles to the cliff edge, and you need to rope up, and move one at a time. You don't know where you are but you need to know where you are. It's dangerous.'

'Is it exciting?' I asked. 'To be in a white-out?'

'Er . . . no, it's a sort of excitement, but I'd say it's more serious than exciting. You need to know what your limits are, what human limits are. However strong and capable you are, there are times when human beings just cannot survive on the high ground of the Cairngorms. It's too bad, it's too desperate.

I was saying to Joe the other day, this always amazes us . . . you can't put it into words, to somebody who's never experienced the severest conditions up there, and convey to them what it's like . . . One rescue I remember, they were two rufty-tufty soldier types, and they went off across the Cairngorms, and on that particular day Joe and I went to the summit of Cairn Gorm, to do a job, it was part of a study we were doing on pollutants in snow. The weather had been cold, and unusually for the Cairngorms there was quite a depth of powder snow. We don't get that much powder snow, you know – we never get the powder skiing you get somewhere like Aspen – it tends to be more wind-slabby, slightly moist, wind-driven snow and it's very dangerous. It comesy-goesy. But on this occasion there was quite a depth of powder snow, and we went into the summit hut, and I can't tell you why, but as I stood in the hut I was really frightened. I could hear the wind picking up, and I've never experienced fear like that, except on one other occasion up there when I was in the avalanche. I was really frightened, and I said to Joe, we've got to get out of here. We must go.'

Even in the retelling her voice sounded urgent.

'What was it about the weather?'

'The weather had changed! The wind had got up to sixty or seventy miles an hour, it was blowing a hooley outside, and all this powder snow was swirling about and it was suffocating! We had to go. So we packed and . . . it was rough. Fighting our way down against the wind. I mean we had a marked route, there were poles, but we couldn't see them. And I said to Joe, if anyone's caught out in this on the plateau it'll be hell! And right enough there were two soldiers out on a three-day expedition. They'd gone across the plateau. They'd dug into a snow-hole and they were on the far side. Now if they'd stayed put, I swear, they'd still be here. But they didn't. They lost their nerve and decided to hack a way out. Big strong lads, maybe they thought, let's get the hell out of here, let's go for it. So they came back over the plateau, in those conditions, and they died. We found them after three days. They died on the cornice, on the edge of the cliffs of Sneachda. I mean not in your right mind should you go up the Cairngorms in bad weather in winter and think you can beat it. You've got to be joking, in winter. I'm years away from the Mountain Rescue days, but I can predict.'

'Tell me about the avalanche,' I said. 'You were once caught in an avalanche.'

She nodded. 'That was in Coire an Lochain.'

'What happened?'

'I was working at Glenmore Lodge at the time. It would have been about . . .' she paused, 'about 1970; it must have been. We were running holiday courses, and on this particular course there were skiers and climbers and on a Wednesday they had the day off, and I took some of them out on a hill-walk. And I knew there was wind-slab. It was one of those years when wind-slab had accumulated on every aspect. It was the way the conditions were shifting and turning, snow falling and consolidating, it was amazing. There wasn't any north–south or east–west slope that was safe, if it had a good build-up of snow on it.'

'What time of year was it?'

'Around March. And it was a nice day, lovely and sunny but windy, blustery, and there was a whizzy loose snow whirling about, up to about waist height, and I remember my dog, my search-and-rescue dog, poor old Barley, having a hell walk. But we were above it. We came over the top of Cairn Lochain and then it was time to descend. Now you know how the ridge comes down, a big broad ridge between the Lurcher's Gully and Coire an Lochain; the plan was to walk down that ridge. There's a steep path that runs down into the bottom of the corrie, from what I would call the col, by two little burns, but I knew we couldn't go down there because the snow wasn't safe. We came down to the col, and I was a few yards ahead of the group, because I was always very careful with students, and I was actually standing on the col, looking across at the corrie, when I felt myself moving. And very quickly it turned into a fiendish avalanche. The whole slope from one end to the other just took off. There was no report, it just went, and it took me with it. I remember the noise was deafening, the crashing of the blocks together was deafening, it was a roar, I couldn't see and I had to get rid of my ice axe. I was going down, and luckily I was able to keep my head up, and I pushed my ice axe off and managed to get rid of it – because in those days we had a wrist loop – and I got that away and just managed somehow to ride the slope down, remaining head up, though I thought I was going to die, there's no question, I couldn't see anything, it was just a maelstrom of noise and snow, and then suddenly it all stopped. And I could see light through the blocks of snow, and I managed to get myself out. And I remember standing, absolutely shaking, from head to foot, and looking across the great mass of debris. It was a third of a mile across, and the blocks were two to three feet thick, and the size of table-tops, and the debris was thirty feet deep. The slope above was gleaming – a sheet of hard ice that the snow had slid off. I could see the others at the top of the ridge. None of them came down with me. They were little black figures across the top. And then Barley appeared from somewhere, poor Barley had come down with me, and he'd got himself out, and I sort of got myself together and we walked out to meet the others, to the carpark. Got on the bus, walked back to Glenmore Lodge. Nothing was said. I'd scraped my arms a bit, but nothing was said. And I went into my room and lay on my bunk, and I could hear the students chatting to each other, and one of them said, 'Oh, the instructor slid down the slope and we walked along the ridge . . .' They were totally unaware of what had happened to me! I mean, I was black and blue from my shoulders to my waist!'

I asked Mollie what she felt about the experience now, so many years later.

She frowned slightly. 'I've forgotten about it. It's gone from my mind. I sometimes read in the newspapers about people in avalanches and I think, I wonder, what would that be like?'

I stayed for half of that hot afternoon by Ciste Mhearad. No one came near, though there must have been hundreds of people admiring the views from the top of Cairn Gorm. The snow lay below me in a quiet mass. I clambered down to the stream flowing from its body. Rinsed my face and hands, pressed my forehead to the ice, saw a thin, pale relic that looked like a bone but turned out to be the stem of a ptarmigan's feather. Smoothed out the bedraggled quills.

6

TO VISIT THE summer snowbeds of Ben Nevis you start in the lush woods at Torlundy – moss, bilberry, pines, birches – and take a path that winds uphill into open country. Here you have a first clear sight of one of the mountain's massive flanks. The impression is of something very physical, as if you are looking at the hunched body of a giant.

I began early, in good weather. A few white clouds eased gracefully across the sky, their shadows shooting over the sunlit ground. The summit of Ben Nevis was hidden by a cloud that was darker and greyer, and also that didn't move; it seemed intent on staying in exactly the same place all day. Britain's highest mountain is said to be in cloud for five days out of six, and one theory is that its name means 'the mountain with its head in the clouds'. Another possibility is that *nevis*, like the French *neige* and the Spanish *nieve*, may have an etymological history that goes back to the original *sneighwh*; if so, Ben Nevis would be 'the snowy mountain'.

In 1818, the twenty-two-year-old John Keats undertook a long pedestrian tour in Scotland and the Lake District in a conscious attempt to acquire experiences that would inspire his poetry. When he came to climb Ben Nevis, on 2 August, he was weary and suffering from a bad sore throat, but his sense of humour was intact. 'I am heartily glad it is done – it is almost like a fly crawling up a wainscot – Imagine the task of mounting 10 Saint Pauls without the convenience of Stair cases,' he wrote in a letter. He and Charles Brown, his walking companion, started about five in the morning – 'after much fag and tug and a rest and a glass of whiskey apiece we gained the top of the first rise'. Later they passed some large snowbeds, and near the top 'a chasm some hundred feet completely glutted' with snow. When they attained the summit they were in a fog that then cleared, but clouds kept sailing by. 'Although we did not see one vast wide prospect all round we saw something perhaps finer – these cloud-veils opening with a dissolving motion and showing us the mountainous region beneath as through a loop hole.'

It was warm enough for Keats to scribble a sonnet, much influenced by the fact that he had been reading Dante's *Inferno*:

Read me a Lesson, muse, and speak it loud
Upon the top of Nevis blind in Mist!
I look into the Chasms and a Shroud
Vaprous doth hide them; just so much I wist
Mankind do know of Hell . . .

These chasms were surely those under Ben Nevis' northern cliffs, in what climbers have since named Observatory Gully and Gardyloo Gully. It's here, late in summer, that snow almost always lies.

The gentleness of the approach to these northern cliffs, following the line of the Allt a'Mhuilinn burn, is belied by what lies ahead. Ben Nevis is a frightening place. It's partly those yawning chasms, partly the unpredictability of the weather. One August morning in my teens I climbed the Ben for the first time, starting in warm sunshine that seemed set to continue all day. Two hours later, halfway up, I was in light fog and a stiff wind; two hours after that, now on the summit, the fog was dense, the wind had become a gale and snowflakes were flying through the air. I looked round – at the dull stones, at the ruins of the old Observatory, at a party of walkers who, bulked out by their clothing, waddled round in the fog like lunar astronauts. I spoke to an Australian in shorts and a T-shirt. He was incredulous. Go up a mountain in Australia, he protested, and it gets warmer! I've never known whether this is true, but it's what he said.

Swiftly changing weather is not unique to Ben Nevis, of course. But the Ben has a special aura that derives from its ancient past as the relic of a vast volcano. Once you know this – once you see that imposing bulk rising from the edges of Loch Linnhe and know that you are looking at the remains of a volcano's inner core – the knowledge becomes critical. You slide back in time, the earth heaves and ruptures, the volcano begins to spit and spark. The Ben's cliffs are contorted and warped and cracked like stuff out of a fiery nightmare; small wonder that Keats' mind jumped to thoughts of hell.

As I walked up the valley, the slopes of the mountain on my left, Carn Mor Dearg, were smooth screes that rose to a flattish ridge. The slopes of Ben Nevis, in contrast, lifted to an irregular barricade of cornices and lips and towers. After a time the Charles Inglis Clark Memorial hut, the base from which most climbers start for the ascent of the northern cliffs, came into view. Here I met another walker. 'Third good day of weather in a row,' he said, 'must be something wrong.' He asked where I was going and I mentioned the snow, at the same time glancing at the cliffs, which were deep in shadow.

Observatory Gully and Gardyloo Gully lie in a steep, scree-lined corrie beyond Tower Ridge, a massive extrusion of gnarled grey rock. With the snowbeds far above me I began to climb, concentrating on the best places to put my feet, occasionally testing the scree with the stub of my walking pole, occasionally pausing to catch my breath. There was lots of parsley fern growing out of crevices, and I picked a sprig. Rolled it in my fingers, held it to my nose. Did it smell of parsley? No, not at all. Half an hour later, I paused again at the sight of a beautiful lichen, an encrusted bloom of hoary grey growing out of a boulder crack; it reminded me of a coral, I could imagine it in an underwater life sprouting from a tropical reef. By now, high in the Gully, I was noticing a quantity of human litter: old gloves, a pair of goggles, bits of climbing equipment, bits of rusted iron, either blown off the summit or discarded by climbers. At this very moment two climbers were roped on Observatory Ridge, one shouting loudly to the other. Their voices reverberated.

I could see the snow much more clearly. There were three snowbeds. One was like the bleached skull of a giant bird. The two further up were right under the cliffs, about 3,700 feet above sea level.

I scrambled towards them. They rested on a steep, forty-degree slope. The larger snowbed, maybe ninety by seventy yards in extent, rose into Gardyloo Gully. Its upper reaches were obscured by the dark summit cloud. The other bed was smaller in length and breadth, but deeper. Its edges jutted some fifteen feet above my head. A blue tunnel had formed in its

body and I crawled in as far as I could go. The blueness shining through the crystals was bright enough to tinge the gleaming faces of the rocks.

When I came out again I stood back, turning on my heels. Elated, awed, the usual things. A little smug. Dozens of people were probably up on the summit, and here I was alone with this icy prodigy. Then a raven croaked and flew overhead, and as the croaking echoed and faded I became conscious of a definite tension.

There are times when summer snowbeds can seem intimidating. It derives, at least in part, from their unresponsive density. While the water of a lake reassures – your thoughts move with ease both across the surface and into the depths – the hard ice of a snowbed is an image of closure and resistance. Then there's the silence. Visit a leafy wood and you hear the rustle of leaves, visit a sandy cove and you hear the break and swish of waves. These familiar, musical sounds are received by

the mind with gratitude. Come in! Stay awhile! Here, instead, a little dripping aside, the silence is profound, and you begin to hunt for sound until you become conscious of the air moving inside your ears. I suspect it is because of the silence that climbers often seem to make such a lot of noise. Shouting to each other on an ascent of some tricky crag isn't merely a matter of communication; it's also an assertion of the human, an attempt to counter the silent power seeping from the mountain. When you add in the hardness of the rocks, the steepness of the slope, the looseness of the scree and the general precariousness it engenders, the feeling of insecurity can become acute. Something hard-wired in the brain begins to mutter away. This is not a safe place, not a place where I ought to put myself. How soft I am – how soft, how fleshy and vulnerable, how puny and insignificant. A fly on the side of an elephant.

I heard a loud sharp clatter from the cliffs above. Whoa, what, a rockfall, where is it coming down? Two, three seconds, another clatter and another, then out of the fog there flies a boulder, black, the size of a, a, a what, a sports bag, a holdall (a holdall?) and crashes down on the upper slope of the snow, bounces with a quiet thud, bounces again and again down the steep face of the snow and then off the snow and with a renewed clattering down the scree slope. Then the noise stops. The silence reasserts itself, even more noticeably than the silence before.

Where one rock falls there could be more. I continue to look up. Smoky vapour drifting round the contours of the crags, like the aftermath of an explosion. The cliffs, grey and fractured like a store of ancient brains. So much violence frozen in these tortured forms. Rivers of fiery matter once flowed here. Now congealed, but still burning inside.

If the boulder had been coming directly at me, would I have had the time or presence of mind to get out of its way? Or would I have been paralysed, unable to move?

I decide not to think about it too much for the moment, and with the tension easing I walk over carpets of green moss to the bird-skull snow. At close range it isn't bird-skully at all. What looked like an open beak turns out to be the entrance to a magnificent ice cave. It's easily big enough for me to stand upright. With its arched ceiling and dank air it resembles a ruined crypt, and in the cave's glossy walls there are niches in shape a bit like the niches in the walls of medieval churches. The ice in the niches is radiant with blue light, and the floor of the cave is covered in glistening black rocks. A hermit, a saddhu, might choose to live in a place like this.

Clamber a little up the cave. Pass an altar-like block of ice. Come to a hole in one wall, a narrow window crossed by an irregular slat of crystal; through it the serrated edge of Tower Ridge and the blue of some sky.

Turn. The view an extraordinary composite of different things. The ice close at hand, the jagged teeth of the cave, the dark cliffs of Ben Nevis, the sunlit pink flanks of Carn Mor Dearg. Cloud shadows the only movement.

Just outside the cave stands a detached block of ice snow with a crest of plated ridges that taper to a point. The spine of a stegosaurus!

Water pouring from the snow crosses a rocky ledge, and then falls in a silver arc to a pool from which another stream issues. I follow it down, my knees creaking. How fine the ice cave was, how atmospheric the clouds and rocks, what a place to visit. All the same, once I'm back in the valley, on easy ground, I'm relieved as much as exhilarated. I dawdle along, enjoying the liverworts and mosses, the burn bubbling in an amiable way, the sun shining on the back of my head. Beyond the CIC hut I meet a walker whose golden Labrador bitch runs towards me, and when I bend in greeting she leaps up and smacks my cheek with a wet kiss.

❄

That evening I get out my lichen book and identify the hoary, coral-like lichen I saw on the climb. *Stereocaulon alpinum*, one of the so-called snow lichens. Great. But I also think a good deal about that falling boulder, I replay its fall a dozen times in my head. I watch myself watching it fall.

The long gap between the sound of the boulder falling and the sight of it falling. The speed of the boulder falling against the inertia of the snow. The blackness of the boulder against the paleness of the snow. The loud clattering of the boulder on the rocks against the soft thud-thud-thud as it pitched on the snow, and the further clattering as it descended the scree. Then that amplified silence after it came to rest.

It's the relationship between the movement of the boulder and the immobility of the snow that interests me. When the boulder first landed on the snow, the snow did not notice, did not respond; it remained entirely impassive. Is that what interests me? Or is it the way the event stretches in my mind? After all, from start to finish, how long did it take? A few seconds?

A few seconds of sound and movement bookended by silence. Is it the pressure of the silence that interests me?

Go back.

The boulder did not come anywhere near me, but the boulder might have come near me. I should have been wearing a helmet. But if I had been hit by a boulder that size, a helmet would have been no protection. Anyway, the boulder came nowhere near me.

Go back.

Why did the boulder fall when it fell? Why did the boulder fall when it fell?

The snow summoned up the boulder. The snow and the mountain knew I was there and summoned up the boulder as a warning. That croaking raven was the first warning. I wasn't welcome.

The snow did not summon up the boulder, the boulder was probably dislodged by some climber hidden in the fog above me. Ravens are common in the mountains, the idea that their croaks are ominous is nothing but an old superstition.

How could snow summon up anything?

If there were a small god, a living presence, within the snow. If there were a small god, deep in the snow but aware of my presence, he might be able to summon up a boulder.

If a small god did live in the snow he might not like being visited. He might be inclined to privacy, strongly inclined to privacy. He would not speak to any visitors, he would refuse to answer questions. If a small god lived in the snow he would prefer to be left alone, not thought about, not written about.

7

THREE DAYS LATER, I and a friend went back to Ben Nevis' northern cliffs and climbed Coire na Ciste, the corrie adjacent to Observatory Gully. There was some snow up high, we could see it from the CIC hut, though how much was impossible to tell. The steep ascent, skirting granite outcrops and a ravine, reached a lochan no bigger than a pond. In the sunshine its water was blue-turquoise and glass-clear. I guessed that it might be six feet deep and I slid one of my walking poles into the water. Ah, no more than three. But further in it might have been nearer six.

We discussed the colour of the water, which reminded me of glacial lakes in the Alps. Such lakes are blue because their water holds a fine silt known as rock flour, produced by the glacier's grinding of the underlying rock. The particles of flour, hanging in the water, scatter the sunlight along the blue spectrum. The silty bed of this lochan was pale gold and patterned with the shadows of the ripples on the surface of the water.

The slope above the lochan, rising to the snow, was an
uninviting chute of rocks and scree, and my bad foot had started
to twinge. I did not feel much like scrambling. But Catherine
was enthusiastic, and when she set off I followed. The climb was
slow, with the scree as loose as a sand dune, and time after time
we dislodged rocks that tumbled downhill, hitting other rocks
with sufficient force to give off a distinct drift of gunpowder.
Eventually we came level with one of the snows. It lay at a
distance, above a scree slope of at least forty degrees, and I
decided it was too tricky to visit. Through binoculars I saw that
it had broken apart in the middle, two large pieces angled in
such a way that they looked like butterfly wings.

The other snowbeds were higher up. They were much
smaller and shallower than the snows that I had seen three days
before, and I inspected them without any great appreciation of
their qualities. The falling boulder was still very much in my
mind, and I glanced apprehensively at the cliffs that teetered

overhead. Far below me lay the lochan, now in dark blue shadow, and beyond it the safety of the sunlit valley.

Many mountain walkers have experienced moments when they have found themselves cowed or destabilised by some hard-to-define emotion. It was a very long while ago that something of the kind first affected me, but I still remember it with great clarity, probably because the experience was so laced with terror. I was nine years old, and it was late on a grey, windy morning. We – my mother and father, my sister Clare and our old dog Bacchus – were on a walk above Glen Affric, contouring in single file along a thin path that followed the side of a steep hill, when the silhouettes of two huge birds entered my vision. Maybe two hundred feet above us, they were sweeping slowly through the air.

Never before had I seen an eagle, although I had long dreamt of such a chance. This same year, back in the spring, a golden eagle had escaped from London Zoo. Goldie stayed on the loose for nearly a fortnight, flying round Regent's Park and its environs, attracting large crowds and causing extensive traffic jams. No one really wanted him to be caught, certainly not me, and I begged my parents to take me up to London to watch him soaring over the park and swooping on small dogs, but they were too busy or too tired, or there was some other reason, and we stayed at home. The newspapers were full of it, however, and when a photograph of Goldie was printed in the *Sunday Times* colour supplement, my father, an occasional weekend artist, decided to copy it in oils. He framed the painting himself, and later hung it in the hallway. Fifty years later it still hangs on the nail that he hammered into the plaster.

With their wing-tips splayed, the eagles in the sky above me now looked black and enormous. In a state of high excitement I fumbled to unzip my anorak and grab my binoculars. These were not good binoculars. They were an old, reconditioned army pair from World War Two with no central focusing wheel, and by the time I had lifted them to my eyes and adjusted each eye-piece both of the eagles had wheeled out of sight. And I couldn't be sure, not a hundred per cent sure. I badly wanted them to be eagles but maybe they weren't eagles, maybe they were only buzzards.

'Can I go and look?' I asked my parents. I was desperate. 'Please.' Yes, they said, if I wasn't too long, if I was back in five minutes, and so, as fast as possible, I scrambled up the brackeny, bouldery slope and arrived on a rocky plateau with my heavily beating heart. In that empty space I was suddenly conscious of my isolation. The eagles were nowhere to be seen. The clouds reeled overhead. I might have been the last person on the planet.

My legs gave way, I sank to my knees, I prostrated myself. I felt myself clinging to the surface of the world as it spun through space. I no longer felt confident in gravity, in that basic connection of my body to the land, and I stretched out my arms to prevent myself from being blown away. Of course, I fairly soon began to recover myself, and then I ran as fast as I could down the slope. The sight of my family, waiting on the path, was wonderful. Bacchus sprang up and wagged his curly tail, while my father removed his pipe from his mouth and regarded me in an enquiring way. I can't remember whether I lied and said that I'd seen the eagles, but I know that I didn't reveal how frightened I had been. We walked on, and before long I was rather pleased and proud, certain that something profound had happened, even if I couldn't say what it was. But it was new, and different. I'd never felt anything like it before.

❄

As I now look back, I am fairly sure that what affected me on that mountain-top was a kind of vertigo in which my brain incorrectly perceived the clouds as stationary and the earth as moving. It drew the mistaken conclusion that the world was spinning at a colossal speed and that I was at danger of being flung off. But I also know that I came face to face with my own mortality. I saw the whole thing, and it terrified me.

It has taken me a long while to recognise this, but death is closely linked to my fascination with summer snow. The death of Bacchus, when I was eleven, was the first death to touch me deeply, and after that there were great-aunts and great-uncles, and a grandfather and grandmother. It was only in my thirties, however, after Clare's untimely death from ovarian cancer, followed not that many years later by the death of my father from stomach cancer, that I began to feel death close at hand.

If this seems an over-melodramatic phrase, another way of putting it might be to say that I was conscious of time passing faster than it had done before. I had two young children, and as I watched them I was anxious on their behalf and thought not only of their unfolding lives but also of my own life. At bedtime I read them stories and poems that had been read to me when I was a little boy, and when it snowed, as it did occasionally, though this was southern England and it never snowed hard enough or long enough, I was pleased three times over: once because I saw the snow, once because I saw their pleasure in the snow, and once because I remembered the wonderful snow of my childhood. But, if I traced time backwards, I now also followed it forwards. I understood my life as a whole, a walk over a strip of narrow land that ended with a drop into nothingness.

Time is in the mind of everyone walking in the mountains. How long is it since I started out, how long will it take to climb that ridge, how long to traverse the ridge and climb those rocks? (Is it time to eat the cheese sandwich in my rucksack?) How long till sunset? Yet there are other timescales. The sun came into existence some four and a half billion years ago and will die in another five billion. The rocks that form the mountains of Ben Nevis and the Cairngorms were born out of fire some four hundred and fifty million years ago. The shapes and contours of the mountains are eleven or twelve thousand years old, carved by glaciers. The lichens on the rocks may live for decades or centuries, their circles slowly widening with age, but most of the flowering plants will be lucky to survive more than a few years. The insects, the flies and moths, have only days or hours left to live. How fast is your heart beating? Feel your pulse. Your heart has been loyally beating since you were in your mother's womb and has never yet let you down, but at some unknown point it will. It will pause as if needing a short break, just having a rest, feeling a bit tired, isn't everyone entitled, oh sorry, didn't mean to frighten you.

Then start again before stopping for a longer break. Then stop for ever.

To live every day like this, thinking of one's heart, collapsing the future into the present, would not be a good idea, but there are moments of sudden perception when different time paths intersect. This corrie, these ancient mountains, this sunlit world, these small flowers, these quiet growths, this shimmering turquoise lochan with its glacial silt. How astounding that a glacier once occupied this ground, how improbable that I should be here on the edge of time, how improbable that I should even exist. How chancy it all is. How easily my life might end with, say, a boulder dropping from the cliffs above.

The presence of cold, summer snow merely heightens the improbability. Snow and time have an equivocal relationship.

On the one hand, snow is ephemeral, a model of transitory existence. 'O that I were a mockery king of snow, / Standing before the sun of Bolingbroke, / To melt myself away in water-drops!' declares Shakespeare's Richard II. On the other, snow is capable of checking the onward rush of time, or at least of giving that illusion. Heavy snowfalls bring the modern world to a temporary halt. Roads are blocked, airports shut down, and there have even been instances when public clocks have stopped. Derry's Clock, in the centre of Plymouth, ceased to function in the blizzard conditions of March 1891, the hands of Big Ben were gummed up by the sticky snow that fell on London on the night of 2 February 1900, and the Town Hall clock at Portsmouth was brought to a halt by the snow of Boxing Day 1927.

Summer snowbeds outlive what would seem to be their natural time. Indeed, writers in the chilly years of the Little Ice Age mention snows that supposedly defied time by lasting forever. The poet John Taylor, who, despite his lameness, walked from England to northern Scotland in 1618, wrote how the flames of Phoebus could never melt the snow; Daniel Defoe, who possibly visited the Highlands in the 1680s, asserted that the mountain tops were 'continually covered with snow, and perhaps have been so for many ages'; John Drummond, in 1737, claimed that the summit of Ben Nevis was covered with 'perpetwall snow'. There were sceptics, however. 'Accuracy of narration is not very common,' Dr Johnson roundly declared, when writing up his Highland excursion in the 1770s (he was querying the supposed fact that Loch Ness never iced over, even in the coldest of winters), 'and there are few so rigidly philosophical, as not to represent as perpetual, what is only frequent'. In 1810 Wordsworth acknowledged that there was 'little of perpetual snow' in the Lake District, and later commentators include C.H. Townshend, the author of *A Descriptive Tour in Scotland*, who wrote in 1840 that the notion of perpetual snow on Ben Nevis was (quoting from *Macbeth*) 'one of those fallacies which keep the word of promise to the ear/but break it to the hope'.

Yet the thought refuses to die. People are drawn towards the idea of the perpetual, and studies of Scottish snowbeds over the past century and a half keep on returning to it. How much snowier was the climate in the seventeenth and eighteenth centuries? How long does a snowbed have to endure before it can be called permanent, and at what point does a permanent snowbed become a glacier? A glacier, surely, is perpetual. Did Scotland's glaciers disappear thousands of years ago at the end of the Ice Age, or is it possible that they survived in some attenuated form as late as the eighteenth century?

Mention of glaciers goes back to the naturalist and historian Thomas Pennant, who travelled through the Highlands in 1769 and 1772. Pennant asserted that two Scottish mountains, Ben Wyvis and An Teallach, contained glaciers. Although this was probably no more than a bit of hyperbole intended to suggest that Scotland's peaks were as worthy of attention as those of the Alps, it set a hare running. Pennant's claim has received support from a 1970s study of lichen growths, which argues that seven of the highest corries in the Cairngorms held glacial ice up to the year 1740. Not everyone agrees. The discussion, occasionally heated and often highly technical, involving the interpretation of soil types and boulder formations, continues to this day.

Why should the history of the Scottish snowbeds be a matter of such controversy, or even interest? We know that the climate warmed in the nineteenth century, and that it warmed still more in the twentieth; the issue is not in serious doubt.

Who cares whether there were or weren't eighteenth-century glaciers? But what fuels the debate is the aching desire for survival. This is why we are attracted to the perpetual. We admire longevity – in trees, in elephants, in bowhead whales and giant tortoises – because we long it for ourselves.

A few years ago I met John Pottie, who was born in 1942 and brought up near the shores of the Moray Firth, not far from Inverness. A short man with a cowl of white hair and kind, almond-shaped blue eyes, he described his first memory of snow. Aged six, he was at school on a cold winter's day. The schoolhouse was a Victorian building with a steep roof, and the classroom had a high ceiling and high windows. He thought it might be snowing but he couldn't see for sure. So he put up his hand and asked the teacher if he could go to the toilets, which were outside. The teacher agreed, and out he went. It wasn't snowing. 'But it must have been in my brain from that time, the snow,' he said.

John wanted to become a meteorologist, but his father, a tenant farmer, advised him that there were no jobs, and he ended up training as an architect in Aberdeen. He missed the mountains, and every winter weekend, along with some other students, he would catch the bus to Braemar and go skiing. They had old-fashioned wooden skis. One fine April they did a two-day-long ski tour across the Highlands, spending the night in a snow-hole. All in all, thirty-three miles of skiing under blue skies. In the summer they went walking and climbing, and sometimes they passed a snowbed. On one such occasion, a fellow student said, 'Did you know that there's a snow patch that lasts all year?' He pricked up his ears.

By 1973 he was working as a council architect in Inverness. His office, on the third floor, had a fine view of Ben Wyvis, which rises to the north of the town. And one day again, this time in May, he was gazing out of the window at the snowbeds on the side of the mountain, and he and two colleagues began to discuss which one would last longest. They took bets, and John made some sketches. Then he recorded the dates on which each of the snows disappeared.

This became something he did every summer. One April, he and a friend, a fellow architect, decided to measure the depth of the biggest snowbed. They carried up a theodolite and measuring staff, and, having found a temporary benchmark on a big slab of rock, took a profile of the snow. Then they went back at the end of August, before the snow had entirely disappeared, and were able to calculate how deep it had been.

I looked at him. 'And?'

'About thirty-six feet.'

'Thirty-six feet? Deep?'

He nodded. 'That's almost the maximum.'

Nowadays the snows on Ben Wyvis almost always melt, John said, but in 1994 one snow looked as if it might survive through to the winter. John hoped and hoped, and when it finally disappeared, on 22 October, he thought, 'Oh no!'

'You mind when the snow disappears?' I asked him.

'Oh, aye! Definitely!' he said warmly. He gave a laugh. 'It's a great joy if you go up there and actually find there's a bit that's still there, when you think it might have gone, it might have gone, and you find it's still there!'

I feel the same. The snowbeds are in a losing battle; the signs are there in the trickling streams that make their way downhill. Second by second, oozing and leaking and dripping, they give ground. Yet the deeper they are the longer they last, and the longer they last the more encouraging it seems. How inspiring that they should have resisted the advance of time until now! Such gritty heroism! It is as if, in a quiet,

determined, single-minded fashion, they are refusing to give in to the inevitable.

Maybe the admiration that they inspire comes from a wider apprehension of loss. Nowadays we are highly attuned to loss, though whether more attuned than our forebears is impossible to know. My eighteenth-century Mouswald ancestors, Jonah and Ann, who lost not only a thirteen-day-old son but also a three-year-old daughter, must have been acutely conscious of loss. Our chances of a long life are much greater than they were back then, yet when loss occurs nowadays we are perhaps less able to cope. The consolations offered by Christianity, among them the prospect of an afterlife, are not, or not for many people, that easy to accept.

There ought to be consolation in the natural world. The narrative of the seasons, the yearly cycle of birth and death and rebirth, the innocence and joy and exuberance of nature, have long been a source of consolation. Now, however, we have a new and much less reassuring narrative about nature, one that describes global loss in the form of disappearing habitats and mass extinction. As many as a hundred and forty thousand species vanish each year, according to a recent estimate. If there were a single cause, it might be possible to fix, but the catastrophes are multiple – scoured seabeds, polluted rivers, bleached coral reefs, chemically saturated arable prairies, industrial smogs, expanding cities, shrinking forests. Time isn't reversible, and it looks as if human beings have now messed things up beyond their capacity to do anything about it and that our world – our one and only world, this blue, floating treasure in which we are lucky enough to live! – is going to hell in a handbasket. (Because there are too many of us, because we are a short-sighted and aggressive species, because people need to earn money, because other people are greedy for more money than they need, lots of reasons, I know. Driving hundreds of miles up to Scotland doesn't help the cause, I know that too, don't tell me!)

Here, however, are these beds of summer snow, stubbornly refusing to conform to the plot, surviving in difficult conditions. Calm down. Take heart.

All that said, I wonder how much environmental loss really has to do with it. Probably not that much, I suspect, or not for me. Loss is key in my response to the snowbeds but it's not global loss. What lies closer to home is more haunting.

8

ADAM WATSON, who knows more about Scottish snowbeds than anyone else, was born in 1930 near the town of Banff in Aberdeenshire. In an early memory, at the age of seven, he is looking through a window and watching snowflakes fall on to a slate roof. Some flakes melt, others stick together and survive; at last, the roof is covered in snow. He goes into the garden and wades in the snow; he is aware of a hush in the town. Two years later he writes a letter about snowbeds to the Scottish naturalist Seton Gordon. In his twenties – by now he is a professional ecologist – he begins to make systematic notes on the survival of particular summer snowbeds in north-east Scotland. At the same time, one or two other like-minded individuals, among them John Pottie, are also tuning in to summer snow and keeping records.

Since the late 1990s, volunteers have carried out annual surveys. One August weekend, generally the third in the month, they do their best to visit all the surviving snowbeds in Scotland.

They take photographs and measurements, and report on the underlying terrain. The survey results are published in the meteorological magazine *Weather*. The ostensible purpose of the survey is scientific, the idea being that long-term monitoring will help build up a picture of climate change. Whether it does so, or whether its findings reflect annual changes in the weather, is a matter of some debate, but the mere existence of such a long-running survey, in which dozens of people take part, is testament to the abiding interest in summer snow.

As a result of this work, we know that the most enduring snows lie not on Ben Nevis, as some nineteenth-century writers believed, but in the Cairngorms. Below the summit of Braeriach lies a great corrie, described in a travel guide of 1894 as 'for solitary grandeur unsurpassed in Scotland', and by Adam Watson, in his 1975 book *The Cairngorms*, as 'a vast super-corrie'. Its name is An Garbh Choire, and only in occasional summers over the past century and a half have its snowbeds disappeared. They are thought to have survived the entire period from 1864 to 1932; they then melted away in 1933, according to a climber who reported the fact to the *Cairngorm Club Journal*. They also vanished in 1959. On 10 September that year, a day of tropical heat, Seton Gordon walked to the corrie: 'Not only had the snow completely melted,' he wrote, 'but even its moisture had gone and there was no trace left of the small streams from the melting snow which usually moisten the slopes below them.' In the famously long, boiling summer of 1976, the corrie's snows just survived – they were rescued by an early snowfall from 9 to 11 September – but in 1996 they had gone by late October, and in 2003 by 23 August. In 2006 the final fragments disappeared between 26 and 30 September. In other words, in the sixty-two years between 1933 and 1995 the snow melted away only twice, while in the much shorter stretch of years between 1996 and 2006, it vanished three times. Since then, the snow has never melted entirely. If there is any snow in Scotland that could be described as close to perpetual, this is it.

The Garbh Choire snow can be seen at a distance from the Cairngorm/Ben Macdui plateau, but paying a visit is a substantial pilgrimage. Whether you start from the south at the Linn of Dee, or from the north via the Chalamain Gap, it takes a minimum of four hours over rough and rocky terrain to reach the corrie. An alternative route, one that might be a little quicker, is to climb the summit of Braeriach and then scramble down the cliffs, but that requires a certain nerve. Even in summer things can go awry if the weather turns. My first walk to Garbh Choire, with my then teenage son, was a debacle: thick cloud came over and lowered itself into the corrie, and although we blundered round in the fog for what felt like an age we failed to find the snow, which was higher than either of us knew. We eventually gave up. The walk back, through driving rain, was very long and tedious.

This time I deliberately picked a blue-sky day without any forecast of cloud. I went from the north, parking in early morning at the Sugarbowl carpark on the road up to Cairn Gorm, and setting off past birch and Scots pines. After clambering through the rocky cleft of the Chalamain Gap, I followed the path over a slope of heathery moorland, and then down into the long pass of the Lairig Ghru. This is an ancient drove road connecting Rothiemurchus and Braemar, but driving cattle and sheep around the heaps of big boulders that obstruct the route must have always been a hard task. The ground is so rough that even walking is quite a trial. 'The summit of the pass and for a mile or two on each side is simply a vast stone-heap, and it is a slow and toilsome process to pick one's way over it,' observed a writer shortly before the outbreak of World War One. Now the sun shone in my face, while the steep and faintly reddish screes – on one side those of Sron na Lairige, the nose of the Lairig, on the other those of Creag an Leth-choin, the Lurcher's Crag – rose 2,000 feet to the sky.

An Garbh Choire consists of two corries, Garbh Choire Dhaidh and Garbh Choire Mor, which are parted by a rocky ridge. Both are spectacular natural amphitheatres – interest in Garbh Choire Dhaidh is enhanced by the waterfall that bounds down its granite cliffs and eventually becomes the great River Dee – and both are good for summer snow, but it is in the bowl of Garbh Choire Mor – 'the big rough corrie' – that the last snowbeds survive. 'This inner corrie is a very secluded place, a holy of holies,' wrote a visitor in the 1920s, 'girt all around with steep slopes and precipitous rocks'. Since the corrie faces east, the snow escapes the warm rain that comes from the south and west, and giant cliffs and buttresses largely shelter it from direct sunlight. The most important factor, however, is the depth to which the snow accumulates in the winter. 'The snae that lies lang lies on ither snae' runs an old Scottish proverb.

Look on a two-and-a-half inch to the mile OS map of the Cairngorms, and you see the pale orange contour lines at the back of the corrie bunched together in a semi-circular curve, and within these orange lines lots of short black squiggles. These impressionistic marks represent the corrie's cliffs, which rise almost sheer to the plateau of Braeriach, a tundra of small stones and gravel. When snow lands on this exposed ground it has nowhere to settle, and the wind whips and whirls it over the cliffs and into the corrie. Here it piles and packs into snowbeds that grow deeper and deeper during the course of the winter. Huge cornices jutting from the cliff edges eventually crash down, adding further snow. In a very exceptional winter, according to one old claim, the snow may achieve a depth of as much as a hundred feet.

As I walked up the Lairig Ghru, I put to one side my eagerness to reach the snow, and instead thought of birds. A 1974 book on the Cairngorms states that ring ouzels 'sing regularly' in Garbh Choire. Ring ouzels are among my favourite upland birds – I can still remember the first one I ever glimpsed, in my early teens, in an abandoned slate quarry round the back of Snowdon, and how for a moment I thought that it was only a blackbird and then saw the ring, the white crescent, on the upper part of its breast. Now, in August, I was too late in the breeding season to catch any ring ouzels in full song, but if a pair had bred in the corrie the parents and their offspring might still be there, perching on boulders. And what of snow buntings? Every summer a few snow buntings fly south from Iceland and Greenland and Scandinavia to breed in the Cairngorms; one was sighted in Garbh Choire in August 1850. What a coup it would be to see a Garbh Choire snow bunting, more than a century and a half later!

Soon after the Pools of Dee, I took a thin path that left the pass and climbed a shoulder of land. Little water courses trickled down narrow channels filled with mosses. Red and gold sundews extended their seductive pads, each one fringed by fronds tipped by gluey pearls. Frogs, their bodies olive-green with black blotches, leapt from under my boots. A pale moth fluttered by, sinking into a hummock of bilberry.

The channels broadened into areas of bog and cotton grass, and in one of these areas there was a puddle of sunlit water crisscrossed by tendrils of bogbean. Fat black tadpoles clustered among the fibrous stalks. Alarmed by my shadow, wiggling their tails convulsively, they scurried to bury themselves in the vegetative sludge. The puddle was shallow, and if it dried up soon, as seemed likely, the tadpoles would probably die.

The path grew more threadbare as it turned up towards An Garbh Choire and for a few brief minutes I had another glimpse of the snow, very white under a blue sky that was made even bluer by my sunglasses. There were several snowbeds, as is usual in late summer. During the past century three have acquired names, Michaelmas Fare, Sphinx and Pinnacles, from the climbing routes up the cliffs; the most westerly snowbed, and also the one that lasts longest, is the Sphinx. It lies about 3,756 feet above sea level.

The path became fainter, and then disappeared completely. I tramped on, dropping down to a burn, where I swished my floppy hat in the water and plonked it back on my head. Then climbed again.

Midway on this long haul from the Lairig Ghru to the corrie there is a tiny refuge of rough stone, an emergency bothy. Here I paused again, seriously short of breath, my legs aching, my heart thudding hard against the wall of my chest. Drank some water and checked my watch, only to find that the face had steamed up. The bothy was not in a good state of repair, the roof broken, the door hanging off its hinges, and inside lay no more than a bench and some scattered floorboards; but on a bad night it would have been better than nothing.

Pressed on. The snows now hidden again, the land rising more steeply, the high sun slanting in rays that showed like smoke against the dark cliffs of the corrie. The contrast between the rugged complications of the granite cliffs, with their furrows and gullies and spurs, and the smooth blueness of the sky became ever more marked. Hard matter, light air. A large green dragonfly fizzed by.

After I had surmounted a great lip of ground, the snow on the cliffs came into view again. At last! I drank it in. On the left, a little plate of sloping snow – then a larger one, that was

Michaelmas Fare – then a much, much larger snowbed at the foot of the Sphinx rock, and still linked by a narrow isthmus to the Pinnacles, good, good – then a small snowbed almost connected to the Pinnacles – then two blobby bits on the right, rather lower. Hmm, not bad. The snow dazzled. The shape of Sphinx–Pinnacles reminded me of a continent on some inaccurate medieval map. I made my usual bad attempt to guess its size, scribbled in my notebook, '80 feet x 20 ???' From the base of Sphinx–Pinnacles a pale channel of snow-melt ran down the scree.

I still wasn't there. To reach the scree I first had to climb a massive rampart of boulders: massive in extent, massive in terms of the size of its boulders. The boulders were frizzling in an extravagance of grey-green and black lichens, and only when I'd crossed them did I see another piece of snow, a beautiful white lake. It was right before me, occupying a gentle slope. The tops of some boulders protruded from its icy mass.

Touched one of the boulders: warm as a stove, melting the snow around it. Shallow snowbeds melt faster than deep ones, and under the hot sun the top of its crusted surface was soft, even mushy. Hmm.

I left my rucksack beside it and climbed the steep side of the scree to the cliff snows. It took me a fair while, maybe half an hour of picking a way before I reached the lower edge of Sphinx–Pinnacles. Yes, I'd underestimated, it was twice as large as it had seemed, and fully ten feet deep. The spread of covering debris was very uneven: some areas, especially the lower right side of Pinnacles, were dark with old snow. Not last winter's snow, but that of the winter before, or the winter before that. It was possible that some of the snow crystals here had fallen back in the winter of 2006–07. How amazing was that.

Yet, as I stood there and consulted my feelings, I was

surprised by a slight disappointment. Yes, I was definitely underwhelmed. Come on, I said to myself, this is heresy, you're in Garbh Choire Mor, wake up, you've been thinking of this for months!

Perhaps it was the strength of the sun. The climb had left me badly overheated and there wasn't a scrap of shade; my brain was simmering. I was sodden with sweat, and my legs were like rubber.

I made more notes, took some photos, and then retreated to the ice lake. There I ate lunch, my back against a rock. Not a soul here, not even a bird. Rolling on to my front, I examined a little colony of lichens. At a range of six inches they were a glade of greeny-grey trees, their trunks covered in bobbles, their trumpet-like heads adorned with scarlet.

Shut my eyes, had a doze. Everywhere the drip drip of the melting snow, and the sounds of water running under the rocks and boulders. Then voices. Sat up, looked round. Nothing.

Another snatch of speech. Two walkers, high on the ridge, maybe a mile away. How still the air was, how carrying their voices.

The silence resumed, the sun beat down, a cloud like an arrow with a stumpy tail drifted overhead. By mid-afternoon, shadows were sliding across the snows. Still unable to shake off a disappointment that I didn't entirely understand, and daunted by the prospect of the walk back, I turned for home. Almost at once my left foot started to hurt. This is what I had dreaded from the very start, months earlier, when I was trying to decide whether to come up to the Highlands. I'd originally damaged the foot in an attempt to get fitter, knowing that I spent too much time at my desk, although also in an attempt to climb out of the black pit in which I found myself that winter, a year and a half after Kitty's death. I ran in a local pine-wood. I hadn't run for decades, but I'd been a good runner when I was a boy, and now I discovered that I could still run at a fair pace for a couple of miles. Only after a fortnight of this new regime did I become aware of strange sensations in my left foot. I returned from a pounding run and realised that the foot was numb, which I put down to the cold weather and the fact that I'd run through some icy puddles. The numbness wore off, but the foot still felt frozen. It tingled with cold. It felt as if the cold wasn't so much on the surface of the skin as deep within the bones. Had I bruised the ball of the foot, perhaps? If it had been a bruise the foot should have soon recovered; but weeks passed and it stayed the same.

So much for the benefits of exercise. A painful foot is not a life-threatening complaint, but nor is it as comic an ailment as it may seem. For much of the time the foot feels wrong; it's as if it has forgotten how, as a foot, it ought to behave. Usually, it's too cold — when the sensation becomes really acute I shove it in a bucket of warm water — but it's a temperamental thing, and sometimes, if I walk on hard city pavements, for instance, it flips in the other direction and feels much too hot.

Now the foot was having one of its hot fits. I stopped at the bothy and put on fresh socks, but they were no help, and after another few minutes I stopped again. This time I bathed the foot in a burn, hoping to block the pain. The foot looked pale and bloodless in the sparkle of water. The heel felt okay, but the bones that led from the toes into the body of the foot were tender, and the front sole, the fleshy pad, was on fire. What was going on in there? What further damage was I doing?

I dried it with a handkerchief and walked down to rejoin the path through the Lairig Ghru. Every step was painful. In the morning I'd scarcely halted at all, but now, under a broiling sun, and over ground covered with rocks that jutted at awkward angles, I made half a dozen stops. When I met a couple resting among boulders on the watershed, I did my best to put on a cheery front. They were walking the entire length of the Lairig

Ghru, south to north, having started that morning from the Linn of Dee. 'Thirteen miles gone, seven to go,' said the man. 'The important thing is to stay hydrated. That's the only thing that matters.' I had a feeling that he might have said this more than a few times during the course of the day. 'Water!' he announced, and glugged from a bottle. The woman, hatless, puce in the face, said nothing.

As I plodded on I thought how they were both a good deal younger than I was, and I began to get angry with myself. This expedition had been a bad idea from the start. Why hadn't I stayed the night in the bothy? Or camped up in the corrie, below the snow? That would have been more sensible. 'But then you would have had to carry a tent.' – 'Well, maybe I should've done.' – 'Maybe you shouldn't have thought of Garbh Choire. Maybe you shouldn't have come up to Scotland at all, that would have been the wise thing to do.' Another voice told me to get a grip and stop complaining, but it was the first, the angry, anguished voice of my foot, that sounded the loudest. 'What are you trying to do, wind back the clock, pretend you're thirty? Face facts: you're too old for this lark.'

Even now, late in the day, the sun was blazing. I followed the valley down. Past the Lurcher's Crag. Up the hill to the Chalamain Gap. There was shadow among the boulders and I wanted to have a long rest but I knew it was better just to keep going, that to stop for any length of time would make things even harder. A hundred steps, pause, a hundred more steps, another pause. It was interminable. Would it have been any easier if I hadn't been alone? I don't know. A last short climb and I crossed the road to the Sugarbowl carpark; by now, eleven hours after starting out, my foot was liquid with pain. I was so dazed that I could barely get the key into the car door. I fell inside, switched on my mobile and texted my son: 'Foot v. bad.

If you ever again hear me propose walking to Garbh Choire in a single day, please shut me in a room for a while. Too old.' He texted straight back: 'Ah I'm sorry. It's miles. Don't do anything tomorrow. Take it easy.'

That night I watched a nearly full moon in the eastern sky and thought of its light on the snow under Braeriach. A good thought. Thinking about the snow was better than being there. I imagined the moon and the snow as sisters, shining at each other. If snow could feel pleasure, this was the time. The contentment of the snow, breathing gently, in the cool of the night.

9

AFTER A FEW days in the Highlands I noticed my attention adjusting a little. My mind's eye, hitherto fixed on the snow, began to focus on plants and mosses. There came a moment one foggy morning when, as I edged round the side of a snowbed, I was stopped short by a most beautiful flower. Inches away, at chin-level, it grew out of a crack in the rock face, a clutch of fleshy green leaves from which a thin, pale-haired, ruby stem offered the world a flower of five clear white petals. The petals had a glistening velvety sheen, and on each lay two dabs of brilliant yellow pollen. The air was still, and tiny fogdrops shone on the tips of five translucent white anthers.

Some mountain plants, like crowberry, with its low profile and woody stems, look tough and resilient – you can easily understand how they withstand the trials of winter – but as I watched the plant trembling in the fog I thought of bone china. Such fabulous delicacy. Such different things in the same moment of perception. Dark rock, pale fog, white snow, white petals.

Starry saxifrage is not at all uncommon, on any walk high in the mountains you stand a good chance of finding it, but many of the plants living near summer snowbeds are rare. Their names are utterly lovely to anyone with a romantic sensibility. Snow rock-moss, icy rock-moss, Ludwig's thread-moss, northern hair-cap moss, snow threadwort, alpine threadwort, alpine lady-fern, Newman's lady-fern, the words of a prayer.

For much of the year plants such as these live beneath the snow, and only as it recedes do they appear and set about the business of flowering and setting seed. In the areas recently left by the melted snow you see little tufts and sprigs of moss beginning to poke into the air, and further away you find stretches of moss greener than any other green, except perhaps waterweed in sunlight. If you stroke them, they ripple like the fur of a cat. I remember one with a pile so thick that it supported fat globules of water, and from its green body grew delicate white flowers of *Cerastium cerastoides*, the mountain chickweed, also known as the starwort mouse-ear. It's a plant that grows only in a few places in the Scottish mountains, often in areas of late snow lie.

I like crouching down and looking as closely as possible. Taking a magnifying glass helps, though it can feel a bit Victorian, and often I make do by inverting a pair of binoculars. Ferns sprouting from damp crevices, rusty-brown liverworts in fancy frills and wavy crusts, lichens like tangled mats of curly hair. Deep wodges of sphagnum, their long strands in shades of washed-out red and pink and yellow. One of my favourite plants is butterwort, a pale green, four-fingered starfish that lives in patches of dark bog. Butterworts are carnivorous, trapping insects on their leaves, which have a slippery texture: shut your eyes and you might be fingering fresh seaweed. They bloom in early summer, each plant a single thin stalk that produces a light purple flower, but in winter they retreat below ground as sleeping buds.

I also like thinking about them. No one before me has ever thought about this gorgeous, velvety moss on the lip of this wet rock. No one has ever wondered at this ring of rusty-red lichen, or this shining star of a saxifrage.

The notion that the best views – the most inspiring, most uplifting views – are panoramic landscapes may still hold sway, but there is a long history of close looking and close thinking. Writing in his mid-thirties, Wordsworth was to conclude his long poem 'Intimations of Immortality' with a singular reflection: 'To me the meanest flower that blows can give / Thoughts that do often lie too deep for tears'; and much more recently the poet Jeremy Hooker coined the term 'ditch vision', which nicely asserts both that a muddy ditch may be worthy of attention – indeed may become the subject of a vision, in the religious sense – and that there is a special type of looking that brings ditches into mental focus. Just as night-vision binoculars help you to see better in the dark, so ditch vision enables you to see the theatre at your feet.

When I was a teenager in a state of infatuation with Wordsworth, I wanted the panoramic views, and thought the end to 'Intimations of Immortality' very weak. Over the years I've changed my mind. That I'm now so interested in detail may be due, in some part, to my short-sightedness: if I take off my glasses, anything less than ten inches away appears in perfect focus. A much larger reason is that I was taught to look at detail by Kitty, who was a botanical artist. On our walks in the Highlands I often found that, while I was exclaiming over a wide-reaching view that involved distant lochs and drifting mist, she would be staring at something close by – a frill of orange fungus, a flaring tuft of cotton-grass, a little fern in a tuck of land.

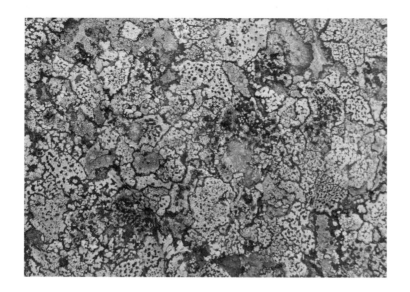

Botanical artists are fixated on minute detail. When teaching, Kitty used to give her pupils a series of preliminary notes that included the following:

> Take time getting to know your plant before you set it up. Such time is not wasted. There is no hurry. It is not a race or a competition. Look at the plant from different angles. Use a magnifying glass if you have one. Examine how the sepals are attached to the stem, for example; how hairy the leaves and stems are; count the pollen grains!

She used to say that the harder you look, the more you see, and the more you see, the more you feel about what you see. You connect emotionally with whatever you are looking at, you empathise with the plant as an individual. If your power of empathy is great enough, you become the plant.

Among the pictures that she most valued was *The Great Piece of Turf*, a watercolour painted by Albrecht Dürer in 1503, when he was thirty-two years old. Now stored in the archives of the Albertina Museum in Vienna, it's a rectangular sheet of paper measuring approximately sixteen by twelve and a bit inches. Painted at a time when art was predominantly religious in content, it is a startlingly secular work. It depicts some common wild plants growing out of a single clod of earth, which could come from a field or from the side of a track. The clod doesn't look as though it has been dug up – it doesn't have sharp edges, as it would if a spade had been used – and the impression is that Dürer has chanced upon it one summer's day. The plants are at eye-level, perhaps three feet away, an apparently haphazard assembly of stems and leaves – some thin, some thick – in a complication of varying greens. Among them are grasses like creeping bent and cock's-foot, and flowers like daisies and dandelions and germander speedwell, but they're not presented in prime condition. The three dandelions have their petals tightly furled. The soil has fallen from the front of the clod to leave a tangle of exposed roots.

This is a study of a particular moment. This is what the piece of turf looks like one day in Nuremberg as painted by me, Albrecht Dürer: a day later, who knows? Rain may be falling, the sun shining, the wind blowing, the dandelions in full flower, the grasses shedding seed. A horse may have wandered up and trampled the turf, a hare may have eaten the grasses. I might decide to paint it differently. Anything. The world is in a state of transience and flux, and if you come back tomorrow (assuming that you're able to come back, for you too are subject to change) it won't be the same. But, for now, this is how it is.

The artfulness of the composition is that it appears artless. At least, this is the illusion that the painting offers: that Dürer hasn't rearranged the plants to improve the composition, or done anything by way of artifice, and instead has recorded what was there before him as faithfully as possible, considering each stem, each blade of grass, each petal. It seems an act of quiet homage to the non-human, which may be a misreading of Dürer's artistic intentions – this was probably a study for some larger work. But, from a twenty-first-century standpoint, the picture does suggest that these ordinary plants, the plants you pass by every day without a moment's thought, are worth attention, they have intrinsic value, they matter.

❄

Snow has no quantifiable value; if you hold a piece in your hands it soon tells you what it's worth by turning to water and running away. Yet this answer is clearly not the final word on the subject, and in the back streets of Scottish history there is an old tradition that puts a particular value on summer snow. Early mention of it comes from Thomas Pennant: travelling in the Highlands in 1769 and staying near Ben Wyvis, he recorded that the chief of the Munro clan, Sir Harry Munro:

> holds a forest from the crown by a very whimsical tenure, that of delivering a snowball on any day of the year that it is demanded . . .

The existence of this strange contractual obligation was confirmed in the late eighteenth century by a local minister, Harry Robertson, who had family connections to the Munros. 'We are assured,' he wrote, 'that a quantity of snow was actually sent to the Duke of Cumberland, in 1746, at Inverness, to cool his wine.' The date is notable. A few weeks earlier, on 16 April, the twenty-five-year-old Cumberland had defeated the Jacobite forces at Culloden, and now he was intent on stamping out any resistance, something he would manage with sufficient efficiency to earn himself the nickname of 'Butcher' Cumberland. One might suppose that the gift of some summer snow, packed in a basket and rushed on horseback to Inverness, was a calculated attempt by Munro to assure Cumberland of his loyalty, but the Munros had long been anti-Jacobite and maybe, as Pennant suggests, it was no more than a piece of whimsy. The tradition has survived; when Queen Elizabeth II visited Inverness after midsummer in 2000, the current chief of the Munro clan, Hector Munro, took the precaution of climbing Ben Wyvis in search of snow. He found some, brought it down and kept it in a deep freeze, just in case the Queen asked for it. (She didn't.)

Eighteenth-century clan arrangements about summer snow seem to have existed elsewhere in northern Scotland. Ownership of Ben Nevis reverted to the Crown if the mountain was ever free of snow, the Grants of Rothiemurchus were obliged to supply the monarch with snow on demand, and the MacIntyres of Glencoe, below Ben Cruachan, held Glen Noe on payment of an annual summer rent of a snowball and a white calf. The Farquharsons were at risk of losing their lands if a snowbed on the Cairngorm mountain of Beinn a'Bhuird ever melted away. This snow is known as 'the Laird's Tablecloth', and the idea still held some of its potency when the laird himself was interviewed in 1982. 'No Farquharson will ever admit that the Tablecloth is not spread,' he declared. 'They might go so far as to say that the linen was dirty and needed a wash, but if you take the trouble to climb up and have a look you'll find it spread, summer just the same as winter!' In recent years, the Laird's Tablecloth has usually disappeared by late summer; only in exceptional years does it survive right through the autumn.

How seriously the idea of a snowball rent was ever taken is hard to say. Was it any more than an aristocratic joke? Would a clan that failed to produce the snow on demand have been dispossessed of its lands? Probably not. Whatever the truth, it's an interesting acknowledgement of the idea that snow may be worth something.

In the 1680s, the great Japanese poet Matsuo Bashō undertook some long-distance walks across Japan and recorded his progress in a series of journals. Bashō was an exponent of Zen Buddhism, and beneath the light, wry tone that he uses to describe his everyday experiences lies a wonderful depth of thought and feeling. What catches his eye are small events in the natural world – blossom, rain, pine-trees, grasses, and also snow. Upon one occasion he attends a snow-viewing party, and a comic possibility crosses his mind:

ichibito / yo / kono / kasa / ur / yuki / no / kasa

Word for word, this emerges in English in a cryptic form:

market-buyers / ! / this / hat / sell / snow / 's / hat

with a looser modern translation as follows:

Gladly will I sell
For profit
Dear merchants of the town
My hat laden with snow

Here we have a neat statement of the clash between two opposing value systems. On one side stands the world of money, and on the other the world of art and spirituality. In offering to sell his snowy hat, Bashō is dramatising his own predicament as a poverty-stricken wanderer who needs money to survive – the hat is itself a kind of poem – while also mocking the notion that we should value things solely as commodities. What matters most in life is beyond money, he seems to be saying. There is the further suggestion, if it's possible to read so much out of so few words, that to find true spiritual fulfilment you need to renounce the material world.

Some of the same sentiment lies behind the snowballs made by the English artist Andy Goldsworthy. In his first snowball experiment, in January 1977, he rolled snow into a large ball among trees in a wood near Leeds. There was a light covering of snow on the ground, and as the snowball rolled along it picked up leaves and twigs and left a dark path. Goldsworthy was interested in the contrast between the dark path and the white ball, and in the relationship between the roundness of the ball and the flatness of the path on the ground. He took a photograph. Other snowballs followed in other winters. He planted a black, peat-covered snowball in the middle of a frozen pond; he built a white snowball high in the branches of a tree; he carried a snowball from high ground to a wood free from snow. With celandines already flowering, the snowball was clearly out of place; even so, Goldsworthy was surprised when a man who happened to be walking through the wood saw the snowball, and kicked it into a stream.

It was after this that he hit on a more subversive notion: that of snowballs in summer. The snowball that he exhibited in May 1985 in a London gallery took three days to melt, and as it did so it released the sticks and seeds and flowers picked up when it came into existence. *Yowdendrift*, an old Scottish dialect word for snow driven out of the sky, was rescued from obsolescence by the poet Hugh MacDiarmid in a memorable line: 'My eerie memories fa' like a yowdendrift' – and I like to think of this melting snowball as an old survivor who was coaxed into reminiscences of the past.

Goldsworthy went on to a much larger snowball exhibition in Glasgow, and then returned to London on 21 June 2000 with thirteen enormous snowballs. He installed them between midnight and dawn in the Barbican area, near one of the world's great financial centres. The chanciness of the project was part of its appeal – the snowballs, not exhibited in the safe surroundings of a gallery but left unprotected in the streets, were vulnerable to the random actions of passers-by. Goldsworthy was curious as to how city workers would react when, in the morning rush hour, they saw the snowballs for the first time. He thought it possible that some snowballs would be destroyed: 'Our urge to make snowballs is matched by our urge to destroy them,' he wrote. He was partly right: the three snowballs outside the Barbican Centre were soon assaulted, while the snowball outside Smithfield Meat Market was pushed into a gutter and then moved to a carpark. Reactions elsewhere seem to have been respectful, although many people wanted to touch the snowballs to check that they were real. A middle-aged businessman poked one of the snowballs with a red umbrella. A mongrel dog stole a stick from one snowball, and carried it away.

There are difficult questions here. Snow is not a commodity that can be bartered or traded: does that make it worthless? Say it is worth something, then what? How do we assess its worth? If, one summer, there happened to be no snow left on the Scottish mountains, would it matter? – Maybe not. – What if there was no snow the next summer, and the next and the next, what if there was never any snow? – No, that too wouldn't matter, because there would still be snow earlier in the year.

What if there was no snow earlier in the year? What if, one winter, as a result of global warming, there was no snow anywhere in Britain any longer – would that matter? – No, that wouldn't matter. Snow doesn't really matter. Other things matter. – Are you certain? – Not that certain. Perhaps it would matter, a little. If there was no snow at all, if there was never any snow, there would be a loss. Something would be lost. – How big a loss? What would be lost? Would it be a loss to other people?

What really matters?

10

IN THE LATTER days of August, I stayed in a log cabin at Corriechoille, with a view that looked beyond conifer plantations to the body of Aonach Mor. At dawn the sun's rays touched the top of the mountain, and edged down its shadowy cliffs until they reached the two snowbeds. With the naked eye they were golden, but through binoculars they had a pink sheen. The pinkness lay under the gold. A thick cloud hung over the back-end of the mountain but above it the sky was pale blue.

I visited the snows later that day. Just over 4,000 feet high, Aonach Mor means 'big ridge' in Gaelic. It rises in the western Highlands above Glen Spean, with Ben Nevis, its neighbour, just two miles away. A tourist operation mars the appearance of its northern slopes, with cable cars swaying uphill to a large restaurant, and a much more scenic though more laborious approach is from the south via Glen Nevis.

I went the lazy way, but after disembarking from the cable car I soon left the crowds behind. I worked my way uphill over

rough ground interspersed with rocky terraces that had to be forded like rivers. In basins of bog, yellow grass flopped like hair over patches of maroon moss. I noted lots of eyebright: toothy leaves, purple stem, toothy white petals each with a blob of yellow flanked on either side by three decorative purple streaks. It was heavy going, and as I rounded a bulge of land and reached the head of a snow tow, a strange construction that reminded me of the watchtower to a prison camp, I startled a merlin perched on a rock. Merlins are sharp, agile little hawks, and a few rapid wingbeats carried it downhill in a low, twisting flight; within seconds it was far away. Oh to be a merlin, I thought. To have hollow bones, to escape this attachment to earth, to slip the moorings and surf the currents of the air, how good that would be.

It took another hour of work before I drew near the two snowbeds that I had seen from Corriechoille. They lay under the cliffs, one higher than the other. I went first to the higher snow. It measured perhaps a hundred feet by a hundred, but in depth it was quite shallow. I then turned to the lower snowbed, and felt my mind begin to whirl. It was in a state of chaos, quite unlike any of the other snows I'd seen. Well, it was a bit like the snow ship on Ben Macdui, but this was much more remarkable. The snow looked as if it had been struck by an earthquake, or shattered by some giant hammer.

I slithered down the wet scree. Every few seconds, still in a state of bewilderment, I paused, but only when I was on its level did I begin to understand what had happened. The upper part of the snowbed lay on a slant of nearly forty degrees, while the lower part was much flatter, almost a bowl, partly encircled by a great bank of rocks. Technically, it's known as a protalus rampart. Green with moss, this rampart had prevented the snow from settling and spreading itself evenly on the side of the mountain, and had also stopped it from melting evenly. In late summer, the weight of the snow in the upper part of the bed had borne down harder and harder upon the lower snow until the pressure grew intolerable. It began to split. Deep cracks, long cracks, developed in the body of the snowbed. These cracks were stress fractures.

How long the fracturing had been going on I had no idea, but it was well advanced. The result was amazing. The snowbed, once flat, had become a jumble of blocks aligned at different angles. The top surface of the snow was covered in tatty brown debris that contrasted with the pure, ultra-clean white of the cracks.

The sharp cracks were like scissor cuts and knife slashes in a swatch of cloth. With my eye, I traced them out and back and out again as though following a tangle of ribbons. Some of the cracks were narrow, but others were wide enough for me to gaze into the depths of the snowbed. There I could see frills, racks, roses, lips, platelets of ice and other unnameable shapes and structures that in their smoothness and fluidity now began to remind me of molten steel. Although they were essentially white, around them flowed a beautiful blue light that was hard to hold in precise focus; it seemed gaseous.

I abandoned the notion of molten metal, tried the insides of seashells, remembered the trumpet flowers painted by Georgia O'Keefe, the startling flesh of coconuts, the ghostly forms that appear in X-rays.

I had an urge to crawl in further, but I checked myself. Too unstable: every so often I could hear not only the usual dripping but also the sound of some shifting chunk of ice.

I climbed round the protalus rampart, went to the bottom of the snowbed. It was a total mess, a heap of geometric ice blocks, the rubble from some demolished house. Astonishing.

Below lay two lochans, from the lower of which a burn flowed downhill, easing past knobbles of greeny-grey land. The light of the burn reflected the light of the sky, across which rafts of pale cloud were slowly moving. Solid, liquid, vapour: water in its various forms.

There had been nothing surprising about the Garbh Choire snows. That was, I think, why my feelings had failed to light up. It wasn't only that I was exhausted; I'd been hoping for too much. But this snow on Aonach Mor was a great and lovely surprise for me. Three times I had been here in late summer, but never before had I seen it like this.

Among the neighbouring mountains to Aonach Mor are the Grey Corries, a chain of peaks named after the colour of their distinctive quartzite screes. A local tipped me off that they still

held some snow. That is, he said, when he had been up there last, he had seen a huge snowbed. Snow occasionally lingers in the Grey Corries, most often in Stob Coire an Laoigh – last year, a big patch had lasted right through the autumn – but by now I'd come to realise that this summer was a very different affair. The weather was still warm and the snow was disappearing fast. I was sceptical. 'When were you there?' I asked. 'About three weeks,' he said, 'there was a lot of it. I shouldn't think it's melted.'

The air was cool and full of moisture. A party of mistle thrushes, their speckled breasts shining, hopped through the rough meadows by the log cabin. I walked up the track and took a right turn into a damp pine forest. Sun slanted between the trunks of the trees, lighting the forest's ginger floor and the bright, dew-laden spiders' webs. Goldcrests were giving little high-pitched peeps, then I heard the irregular, rattling calls of a lesser redpoll, then the keening cries of a young kestrel. I came

to a dam, and above that a burn flanked by birch trees; as I crossed, jumping from one stone to another, a small bird flew very straight in my direction, low over the water. Wings whirring, small, brown, white on the throat, a dipper . . . would it fly past me – no, no, it had seen me, it was swerving away, turning, shooting back the way it had come.

There followed a long slog up a steep, brackeny slope. Bog asphodel, a few faded orchids, a pair of red grouse that burst from the ground near my feet and made off with machine-gun calls. At last I was up on a broad hump of land under a fleecy sky, and now I saw the Aonach Mor snowbeds again. Against the body of the mountain they looked small and vulnerable. Further away, several snows on the northern flank of Aonach Beag were falling into shadow. They too looked small, but it was hard to tell at a distance.

A herd of sheep bunched and stared. A ewe stamped a foot. Then a party of six or seven birds flew up, flashing pointy wings. Golden plover – dotterel – one or the other – damn, they'd gone. Which would I prefer them to be? Probably dotterel, but golden plover had been my first thought.

When I reached the first of the Grey Corries I looked into the bowl under the scree. No snow, none at all, although I could see across to Stob Coire an Laoigh. Where the snow must have lain there were sheets of brilliant green moss. I continued along the mountain ridge and looked into the next corrie, which was also snowless. My information was out of date.

I turned back, not that disappointed. The snowbed on Aonach Mor had been so interesting that it would have been unreasonable to be disappointed, and the Grey Corries are a fine place to be on a summer's day. Yet, not for the first time, I found myself wondering just how many snowbeds would survive into the autumn. The Observatory Gully snow on Ben

Nevis, and the Garbh Choire snow would surely be okay, but for all the rest it would be a close-run thing. Even the snowbeds on Ben Macdui might disappear.

On the descent, I chanced upon what for me is the most jaw-droppingly beautiful of wild flowers, grass of Parnassus. The two colonies were growing near some sparse patches of bracken, a few hundred feet above the burn; I'd missed them on my way up, and if I'd taken another way down I would have missed them again. Now I settled to look at them.

Different explanations have been advanced as to why grass of Parnassus should be so called, but the probable truth lies in a passage in Book 24 of Pliny the Elder's *Natural History*. Pliny describes a grass on Mount Parnassus with ivy-like leaves and a white, scented flower; to cattle, he says, no other flower is more attractive. He adds some sentences about its medical properties, including the information that its seed is an effective remedy against dragon bite. Printed editions of Pliny were widely circulated in fifteenth- and sixteenth-century Europe, and the name 'grass of Parnassus' appears in an English herbal of 1578. Linnaeus stuck with the idea when he gave the plant its Latin nomenclature, *Parnassia palustris*, in the eighteenth century. However, it's not a grass, and it seems very unlikely that *Parnassia palustris* is the same as the plant described by Pliny. Nonetheless, Mount Parnassus is the legendary home of Apollo and the Muses, and it feels an appropriate name for a flower of such divine qualities. According to one legend, it was the favourite plant of the sixth-century Christian missionary St Moluag, who travelled extensively in Scotland and founded a monastery on the small Hebridean island of Lismore.

Grass of Parnassus is commonly found in the north of England and Scotland, not only on damp hillsides but also on sand dunes. What's so special about it? This is one of the places where language struggles, just as it struggles with snow. It has dark green, heart-shaped leaves, with the stem growing out of the top of the heart and rising for some eight inches. Its petals, five in number and evenly spaced, are meringue-white, and grooved with very delicate thin lines that look pale grey or green, or grey-green, though there is also a great deal of white in the colour. The colour in the grooves darkens slightly towards the inner part of each petal and lightens towards its outer edge. The five stamens are a different, more creamy shade of white. When they unfurl and extend very straight they are like the spokes of a wheel, and on the end of each luminous spoke there is a little blob of darker cream. The most ravishing feature is that the plant possesses another, lower wheel, composed of five miniature limbs called false stamen, or staminodes. In their translucence and stubbiness they are a little like the hands of frogs and toads, but the fingers are long and slender, and each one is tipped with a shining globe of gold.

The beauty of the plant lies not only in its detail but also in its symmetry, its decorativeness, its modesty, its subtle coloration and the way its various parts seem so wholly in harmony with each other. That is to say, its beauty lies in its order. As human beings, we are deeply drawn to order precisely because we live in a world characterised by violent disorder. In religious terms, contemplation of grass of Parnassus suggests that the entire universe is fundamentally ordered, which in turn suggests that there could be an ordering force, a god; this is what William Blake seems to argue when, in the early nineteenth century, he writes of seeing a world in a grain of sand, and heaven in a wild flower. God was out of sight but never far away; the natural world was infused with His presence.

Can we really see heaven in a wild flower? A contrary view

to that of Blake was articulated by William Carlos Williams in his 1940 poem 'Raleigh was Right':

What can the small violets tell us
that grow on furry stems in
the long grass among lance shaped leaves?

Glance at the history of the past century and it seems a good question. Shouldn't we wake up to reality? Williams is saying. Give up this romantic nature worship, abandon this quest for the divine, this endless rapture: it won't help any longer.

Still, I spent a long time with the grass of Parnassus, engrossed by its approach to perfection. The fact that I had failed to find any snow seemed unimportant.

Before dusk that evening the wind picked up but close to the ground there were patches of quieter air. Near the log cabin, a low white cloud seeped slowly down the side of a hill partly planted with conifers: as it descended it appeared to be rolling like a fluffy cylinder. Parts of the cloud refused to hold to this cylindrical form and erupted in gentle tufts and plumes that hung bending and curling for a few seconds in front of the dark conifer belt before they were carried away. This too I found very beautiful, although it was not in the least ordered.

11

KITTY'S WORK AS an artist changed with the diagnosis. She had always depicted plants that weren't necessarily in prime condition – snowdrops rising from wads of leaf litter, old twigs tangled in flowering ivy – but now she became intensely interested in decay and regeneration. Soon after recovering from the first mastectomy, she produced an intricate study of an ancient hedgerow that had been savaged by a mechanical flail. The blades of the flail had sliced deep into the hedge, and its branches had been torn and smashed almost beyond recognition. She worked on the drawing for months, completing it before, as she wrote, 'the nettles, shining cranesbill and other plants within the hedgerow grew up to engulf its wounds and disfigurements'. Shortly after that, she drew *The Viable*, a picture of forty-two acorns that had fallen from a single oak. Forty-one of the acorns were infected by wasp galls, a parasitic infection that destroys the healthy tissue; but one acorn had escaped infection, and would be capable of growing into a tree.

Her last picture, a drawing of three greatly magnified pine cones that had been nibbled by wood mice, was entitled *Some Are More Eaten Up Than Others*.

These and her other late works have a particular beauty. They express a vision of the world as imperfect and disordered, accidental and dynamic, with life and death constantly challenging each other. I came to see them as profoundly autobiographical, almost as self-portraits, but it wasn't until after she died that I understood what she was doing. I now think that they are outrageous statements of resistance. I think that as she worked on them, hour after hour, day after day, during those years of illness – pictures like these take a very long time – she was engaged in a high-wire act of bravado. Each tiny ink mark on white paper was an affirmation of life.

No doubt all this plays into my complicated responses to summer snow. There are times when I imagine the snowbeds as shrines and chapels, scattered in the mountains, the relics of a disappearing religion, and there are other times when they fill me with ideas about beauty and death. Death robs life of meaning, beauty infuses life with meaning. Death and beauty are aspects of the polar divide: on the one side weight and matter and inertia, on the other light and spirit and the airy zones. Summer snow is a bridge that stretches across the divide.

It would be wrong to give the impression that, during these long walks, I had nothing else in my head. Far from it. I was in the mountains for the greater part of every day, and one recurrent thought was that perhaps it was a mistake to think about snow quite as much as I was doing. Unrelated things kept breaking in. On those visits to Ben Nevis, I twice passed the CIC Mountain Rescue hut. To its door a metal plaque is affixed, inscribed as follows:'This hut is dedicated to the memory of Captain Charles Inglis Clark died of wounds Mesopotamia 6th March 1918'.

Mesopotamia, the land that lies between the Tigris and Euphrates rivers, is now divided among several countries, chiefly Iraq and Syria. It has long been contested territory, and during World War One was the scene of fierce fighting between the armies of Britain and Turkey. Clark was buried outside Baghdad. His father and mother, both noted mountaineers, paid for the building of the memorial hut, which was formally opened in 1929.

Is it harder to erect a wall round one's attention than it was? I don't know, but I'm not able to shut out the bad stuff, not entirely. Nor, in the end, do I want to; something in me resists the idea of erecting a barrier against the world. I don't want to use nature as a safe area into which I retreat when the rest of life gets tough. I don't want to stop reading newspapers or listening to the radio.

Late one afternoon, after walking in the mountains, I bought a newspaper that printed a photo from the Syrian city of Aleppo. The city was the central focus of fighting in a civil war that had run for years, and the photo showed a five-year-old boy whose home had been blasted by a bomb. He was lucky enough to have been rescued. Someone had hauled him out of the wreckage and carried him to an ambulance, where he had been put in an orange chair that was too big for him. Here he was, deep in shock, in shorts and a T-shirt, his legs sticking out, one side of his face dark with blood. His skin and clothes were grey with dust, as if the blast had sucked the colour out of him. His eyes were open but seemed unseeing, as if he had lost the ability to see. While the power of the image came from that unfocused gaze and all it said about his innocence, it was multiplied by the mismatch between his own size and the size of the chair. He was not only in a chair that was too big for him, but in a world that was too big for him.

Many children have died in the Syrian war, and a photo like this ought not to have been a surprise. Although I was disturbed and angry, I was also suspicious of my emotions: how easy it is to be disturbed and angry, how difficult (how impossible) to do anything about it. Nonetheless, when I watched an evening TV news bulletin, one that carried a short piece of video footage showing the boy as he was lifted into the ambulance, the pressure of the emotion remained intact. I did not wake in the night and find the boy's dark eyes looking at me, but the pressure was there.

There is a poem by Derek Mahon called 'The Snow Party'. Published in 1975, when Northern Ireland was engaged in its own civil war, it is a powerful rebuke to those who avert their gaze.

Bashō, coming
To the city of Nagoya,
Is asked to a snow party.

There is a tinkling of china
And tea into china;
There are introductions.

Then everyone
Crowds to the window
To watch the falling snow.

Snow is falling on Nagoya
And farther south
On the tiles of Kyōto;

Eastward, beyond Irago,
It is falling
Like leaves on the cold sea.

Elsewhere they are burning
Witches and heretics
In the boiling squares,

Thousands have died since dawn
In the service
Of barbarous kings;

But there is silence
In the houses of Nagoya
And the hills of Ise.

While Mahon is replying to Bashō, and implicitly criticising the philosophy of detachment from worldly things, he is also invoking the last lines of James Joyce's short story 'The Dead', where the snow, falling over the whole of Ireland – 'falling on every part of the dark central plain, on the treeless hills, falling softly on the Bog of Allen and, farther westward, softly falling into the dark mutinous Shannon waves' – seems to hold out the possibility of a universal peace. Here, in contrast, there is no ceasefire, no peace. Here we see the houses of Nagoya where the middle-class guests sip their tea and admire the snow, and there we see the boiling squares in which the heretics and witches are burnt.

How can one reconcile the beauty of snow with the horrors of Aleppo? What can the old snow, hiding in the shadows of the Scottish mountains, possibly tell us that might be of any use? When I revisited some of the romantic ideas that

I'd been entertaining, I felt queasy. Suggesting that snowbeds could be images of how to live in a difficult and hostile world seemed fatuous. What was I doing here?

Thoughts like these can be held at bay for a while, but I noticed that I did not throw away the newspaper, and I began to wonder if it wasn't time to go home. I'd seen most of the snowbeds that I'd hoped to see, and the memories would carry me through the winter and beyond. There was stuff I needed to do at home – post to answer, bills to pay, a garden running riot. Yet I was aware of a great reluctance to leave the mountains. Instead of becoming more tired, I had been energised by the walking. My fear that I would be unable to keep going for hours every day had been unfounded, my back had been no trouble at all, and although my left foot had never stopped grumbling, it had soon recovered after the Garbh Choire walk. The different snows that I'd seen, especially that fantastic assortment of debris on Aonach Mor, seemed to have given me a new charge: I was fitter, younger, more alive. I wanted to see more snow, if possible.

So I put aside my reservations, and stayed in the Highlands a little longer. One day in early September I returned to Creag Meagaidh. The wind had shifted to the south-west and the weather was now uncertain. Flying clouds, pale sheets of rain sweeping across the hills. There were moments when it was still summer and others that felt like the edging-in of autumn. Swallows continued to dip over the meadows, but the willow warblers had fallen silent, and the leaves on the birch trees were spotted with decay. Fluffy seeds blew from the heads of withered marsh thistles. By the path leading up the valley stood a large fly agaric toadstool, the top surface of its cap a gleaming, sticky pink. When I touched it with a finger it wobbled, and the gills on the underside were loose and flaky as the flesh of overcooked fish. A fungus in its last days.

After the no-show in the Grey Corries I was far from confident that there would be any snow left, and as the path led towards Coire Ardair I kept glancing up. The high, rugged cliffs, dull under the cloud, swung into view. Two thin white waterfalls, thread-like, plunged towards the lochan. Then I caught sight of something whiter, the edge of the lizard snow in Raeburn's Gully. Still there! I felt a lift of the heart. It didn't look big, but it hadn't completely gone. What of the other piece of snow, the beautiful, shining slab that I'd sat and watched? No, that had disappeared.

It was raining. I stopped, put on overtrousers, a hat; then rounded the lochan and climbed until I reached a good vantage point. There I stopped, heaved off my rucksack, sat on a grassy ledge and looked up at the gully. The lower part of the lizard had gone, and all that remained was a section of snow near the very top of the gully. The slope on which the snow rested was very steep, so steep that it seemed strange that it should not have slid down.

Wondering whether some boulder supported its base, I fished out my binoculars. Then I was taken by surprise. The snow was no longer anything like a lizard. It was now human in shape. It had a round head, a neck, a body. The right arm was buried in rock. The left arm was missing, amputated somewhere below the shoulder. The flaring torso was draped in a dappled white robe that reached to the ankles.

Of course, it was too big to be human. Much too big. If it were that big, it would be the body of a giant. And the head was too small for the body. Yet the angle at which it lay was the angle at which a human might lie after an accident, and when I noticed a fissure in the torso I thought of broken

classical statuary. The *Venus de Milo*. The tyrant Ozymandias. Or was this Lenin, sometime after the end of the Soviet Union, toppled from his plinth in a public square?

Then it came to me: this is an angel, one that miscalculated. Skimming the crags, it had been caught by an unexpectedly strong gust of wind that sent it flying into the rocks. I was looking at a white angel that had fallen and crashed into our failing world.

How curious the way the mind works. Why should I find this such an attractive proposition? Because my interest in the survival of the snow was all about the survival of the spirit, or the idea of the spirit in a world of matter? Maybe. Wasn't I simply using this passive, inert snow as a landing strip for my own fears and hopes? As I had been doing all month? Maybe.

Still, I couldn't get away from it. A broken angel. It had no chance of lasting through to the winter. No chance of salvation. That it had survived this long was good, however, and I was pleased to have seen it.

12

TWO DAYS LATER the air was warm, humid, even sultry. My car's temperature gauge gave a reading of twenty-five degrees, and it felt hotter. Nearer thirty, I thought. Yet a murky cloud hung over the Cairngorm plateau, and there was a high wind blowing. The Mountain Weather Information Service warned of fifty m.p.h. wind speeds. 'Buffeting,' it said, 'will make walking difficult . . .'

I spoke to one of the Cairngorm rangers. 'It's orographic cloud,' he said. 'Perhaps a good day to walk somewhere else.' Orographic clouds typically form on mountains in conjunction with a warm wind. 'No,' I said, 'I particularly want to go to look at the snow.' He said, smiling, humouring me: 'Well, it'll still be there tomorrow.' (Ah, but will it? I thought. How can you be sure?) He pulled out a sheet of paper showing the forecast for the next day; it was possibly a bit better, but not much. 'It might clear,' he said. 'But not today. Today's not the day.'

I drove to a café by Loch Morlich. Opened my laptop and looked again at the forecasts. The Met Office said that the fog would lift by five in the afternoon, but that was too late. If I was to visit all the snowbeds on the plateau, I needed at least four hours, probably five. I needed to go now or not at all. I dithered. I looked up at the plateau: still in heavy cloud. I drank a second cup of coffee, went for a stroll by the loch. Why was this so hard to work out? The ranger was right, it wasn't a day to walk on the plateau. Leaving it till the morrow was much the most sensible thing to do.

But I didn't want to leave it, I just didn't. I felt something was happening up there right now.

I'd been anxious at the very start of the trip, back in early August, as I drove up to the Highlands without knowing what lay ahead. Then, once I'd found the first snowbeds, the anxiety had subsided. Now it was back and in a much more acute form. I didn't understand it entirely, but my mind felt frayed. Time was shooting past, things were slipping away. What if I went just to Ciste Mhearad? That was the easiest snowbed to reach. An hour or so up, an hour down. I could manage that, surely.

Drank more coffee.

Ate lunch.

In mid-afternoon I packed my rucksack and drove back to the Cairngorm carpark. Put on my boots and began to climb for the umpteenth time. Soon I met a pair of walkers on the way down. 'It's sixty-mile-an-hour up on the plateau,' said one of them, a chunky type who looked me over in a quick assessment of my age and physical capabilities. – 'I thought it was meant to be only fifty,' I said. – 'No, it's sixty,' he insisted, 'it's not easy to stand, we were almost blown over this morning.' – 'Tomorrow'll be better,' his companion chipped in. 'We were on our knees.' I understood: they too were warning me, they didn't think it was that safe, they thought I ought to turn back. But by now the decision felt irrevocable: this was it, today was the day, tomorrow would be no good.

Climbed on. Came to the restaurant below the summit of Cairn Gorm. Yellow diggers and other heavy machinery beeping in the fog, repairing the snow fences, preparing the slopes for the winter skiers. As I passed the end of the ski tow I saw a wheatear grounded by the force of the wind. My anorak and overtrousers flapped away but it was walkable, I wasn't on my hands and knees.

The knot of anxiety within me had tightened, however. Three and a half weeks, weeks of warmth and sunshine, had passed since my last visit to Ciste Mhearad, and I had no idea how the snowbed might have fared. It might have vanished, I knew that. The year before, it had survived until 29 November; the year before that, it was gone by 1 September; the year before that, by 5 September, the year before that, by 4 September.

Now it was the 5th. I neared the edge of the bowl. Looked down.

Goodness. Oh. Oh no. Some snow, not much. Not very much at all.

Among the ruins stood another walker, a bearded young man.

I picked a way down to him. The wind eased as I descended the slope. I said: 'Still some left.'

He said: 'Yeah, it's amazing.'

'There was much more,' I said. 'Three weeks ago there was much more.'

I was in a state of high emotion. I swept one of my walking poles to indicate the full extent of the old snow, as it had been three weeks earlier.

He said: 'Amazing things. Could last until the winter.'

I didn't want to sound negative. 'Perhaps,' I said.

Perhaps yes, but perhaps not. This warm air was like a big hair-dryer.

'Depends how long before the next snow,' he said.

'Yes,' I said.

When would the next snow fall? The trouble was that the next snow, even if it came soon, would probably be no more than a light shower. It would dust the mountains and then melt. To save the snowbed, a heavy fall was needed. An old Scottish word for a heavy fall of snow is an *on-ding*, a *ding* being a blow. 'Look out, Jock; what kind o' nicht is't?' the Laird of Dumbiedikes asks his son in Sir Walter Scott's *The Heart of Midlothian* (1818), and receives the succinct answer: 'On-ding o' snaw, father.'

The next on-ding of snaw might come in a week's time, but the middle of October was more likely. Or late October, or early November. Much, much too late.

The bearded guy looked towards the plateau. 'What's it like up there?'

'Blowy. Not too bad. Better down here.'

'Okay.'

He shouldered his pack and went on down to the shores of Loch Avon, where he was planning to camp out of the wind. I did my usual pottering. The snowbed at Ciste Mhearad had broken into ten disorganised chunks. The largest was maybe twelve feet long and twelve feet wide and two-and-a-half feet deep. The next largest was half that. The rest were much smaller. I noticed a short tunnel, and a nice little bridge of crystals, but all I could think was how big and glamorous the snow had been less than a month before and how disappointingly small and unglamorous it was now. I'd

expected at least one substantial block, a body of snow, not this dismembered litter.

That wasn't all. The snow had lost its inner light. It didn't sparkle or glow, it had given up the fight, or so I felt. It was a passive thing, resigned to its fate. The rats of the summer heat had gnawed its body, and now it had lost the will to defend itself.

If a small god had been here among the snow, just suppose; if a small god had been living here all summer, quietly thinking, quietly hoping, he was long gone. He had packed his bags and departed in dismay.

As I skirted the flanks of Cairn Gorm and headed for Ben Macdui I was surprised to find my legs heavy. And not only my legs: my mind was sluggish and unresponsive, and when I came upon a flock of fifteen ptarmigan I felt scarcely a thrill. They shuffled out of the way, declining to fly. Such fine birds, what was wrong with me? Then, through the fog, as I plodded along the thin path that leads south from Coire an t-Sneachda, I saw the final remnant of the Coire Domhain snowbed. No more than a foot deep, a fragment, it stretched over the dark ground like the pegged-out pelt of some animal.

Dutifully I cut down. Examined it like a forensic scientist. Tried to admire its contours. The glory had gone, however. I couldn't believe how quickly it had melted, and with it my enthusiasm. Suddenly I asked myself whether I wanted to traipse across to Ben Macdui. I'd been here too long, hunting round these old, dying snows; it really was time to pack it in and go home.

Crouched in a lee of land, ate an energy bar, wiped the lenses of my glasses. There was a moment when the cloud lifted and a stretch of the great cliff that rises above Loch Avon appeared. Then the cloud lowered itself again and the cliff vanished. The wind was still blowing hard.

No, I knew, I had no strong desire to climb down the cliffs and inspect the snowbeds in their final days. I didn't think they would have disappeared but they might have done, and I couldn't face it. Not in cloud, not in this wind, not alone, not with evening approaching, the prospect was too melancholy. But I wanted something to take from the day, and I decided to cross the plateau to its western edge, hoping that the cloud would lift enough for a view across the Lairig Ghru to the snows of Garbh Choire. The great snows of Garbh Choire, under Braeriach. They would be still there; I was sure of that.

Plod, plod. Reached Lochan Buidhe; the wind sent wavelets scudding across its surface. Walked south-west for a quarter of a mile, over bare ground, gravel, rocks.

There I halted. This was the best vantage point. The fog had been thinning for some time and now it lifted decisively from the plateau. I raised my binoculars and looked across the gulf of air towards the low sun. The evening light was polarised, the shadows profound. Shadow upon shadow upon shadow, each one adding an extra layer of obscurity. Without binoculars it would have been impossible to see through them.

Yet I could see enough. There was still cloud on the top of Braeriach, a flat band of cloud on the ridge, but beneath it no snow, none at all. I was staring right into the smoky-blue heart of the corrie and there was not a sign of snow, and I felt a moment of panic, Christ, surely not, surely not. Then I told myself to stay calm. The lovely snow at the base of the cliffs must have melted, but the other snows, the Sphinx, the Pinnacles, were hidden in the cloud. I visualised them on that boiling day, high above the scree slope on the right of the corrie. Well, I could see the scree through my binoculars, but not the cliff above the scree. That was where they were, hiding. I would wait for a few minutes. If the cloud lifted, it lifted; if not, so be it, I would head back.

Knelt and waited with the wind full, ruffling the grasses in front of me. Turned to look over my shoulder. The summits of Cairn Gorm and Ben Macdui were now clear and sunlit. I wondered if, at this moment, Braeriach was the only mountain in Scotland with its head still in cloud.

Above the cloud the sinking sun blazed in my face. A disintegrating swirl of white vapour with an iridescent peacock tail slid up from the Lairig Ghru and poured away. Then another. The grasses shone in a foxy ginger of astonishing intensity.

Minutes passed, and more minutes. Evening was fast coming on, by now I was possibly the last person on the plateau, but I couldn't bring myself to leave. It was ridiculous when I knew the snowbeds had to be still there, they couldn't have melted, they hadn't disappeared for years. How deep they had been! It was impossible. Yet I knew that it wasn't impossible. The warm weather had reduced Ciste Mhearad to a few pitiful lumps and it might have done the same for those of Garbh Choire.

A chink of light. The cloud had briefly lifted from the ridge to the south of the summit, near Sgor an Lochan Uaine, the Angel's Peak. It sank back, but I was encouraged, surely the wind would blow it off soon. Yet it might not. Orographic cloud is persistent stuff which the wind, paradoxically, holds in place. For the cloud to vanish, in all likelihood, the wind needed to drop. This wind was as strong as ever; it was a gale.

So here I was, on my knees, late one day in the summer of 2016. My heart in my mouth. Absurd. Is this what it had come to? It: me, the world, human history. The winter would bring more snow, so why did it matter, it did not matter, not really, not at all, the old argument raged away in my head, but at that point it mattered at least enough to keep me there. I needed to know if the snow had survived. If I didn't find out now, maybe I'd have to spend another day hauling myself up the Lairig Ghru and climbing into Garbh Choire, and I knew I didn't want to do that. But now the ragged lower edge of the cloud on Braeriach was lifting again, and for an instant I seemed to see them, three veiled shapes, I wasn't sure but then I was, two large, one small, I'd seen them, they were fine. Then the cloud was down again. But what an idiot to have doubted, of course they were there. Holding out until the weather turned and the first snows of the new winter fell. Oh good, good, good, a thousand times good.

I walked back over the plateau, altogether happier, my step light and springy on the soft ground, as if gravity itself had let up a little. The wind was now on my side, pushing me along, helping me on my way. As I passed the cairn where I'd seen the solitary vole on that first day, I thought of friends and family, and how much they really did matter. What would it be like to go through the world alone? I even had a snow-related thought: that ice was water pretending to be a rock. No, ice was water trying to be a rock. Trying and failing, but trying. As humans yearn to escape gravity and fly like birds, do rocks ever yearn for the fluidity of water?

Then the idea of melting rocks came into my mind and I remembered Burns' tender poem of farewell, his pledge of eternal love:

As fair art thou, my bonnie lass,
So deep in love am I;
And I will love thee still, my dear,
Till a' the seas gang dry.

Till a' the seas gang dry, my dear,
And the rocks melt wi' the sun,
And I will love thee still, my dear,
While the sands of life will run.

The sun was even lower now. As I bounced down the shoulder of Coire an Lochain it disappeared behind the bulk of Creag an Leth-choin, the Lurcher's Crag, and then reappeared. My shadow stretched long over the rocks and the grasses were a carpet of gold. Soft, gentle light. Below, in the Spey valley, lay the bright, shining eye of Loch Morlich and the dark pines of Rothiemurchus, and then line after line of hills that faded into the evening haze, and above the haze there were little white clouds like distant islands and above them the sky was turning an ever paler blue, and I went beyond exhilaration and became filled with the sense of blessedness: how blessed I was, how blessed to be alive. Shortly before reaching my car, which sat alone in the carpark, I pulled out my mobile and rang my son and daughter. 'How are you?' they said. – 'I'm very well!' I said. – 'How's your foot?' they asked. Finally, after so long, I had forgotten the foot.

Author's Note

I am enormously grateful to Richard Kerridge for scrutinising an early draft of this book, and for forty years of friendship and conversation; to Paul Wakefield, for his exceptionally generous advice and help with the photographs; and to Catherine Simmonds, for her insight, sympathy, kindness and much more. A very long time has passed since I talked to Cyril Abel, Willie Anderson, Peter Lightfoot, James 'Tosh' McIntosh, Professor Elizabeth Morris, Paul Noble, John Kinnaird, Mollie Porter, John Tweedie and Adam Watson about snow, but I should like to thank them warmly; especial thanks are due to John Pottie, who was good enough to accompany me on a long walk up Aonach Mor on a day of fog and drizzle. Alistair Forsyth's ornithological enthusiasm has spurred me on since we were at school together, and I owe him a lot. A very big bouquet of gratitude goes to my excellent agent Isobel Dixon, and another to Hannah MacDonald of September Publishing for her faith in the possibility of a book on summer snow. I am indebted to all those at September who have helped, among them Charlotte Cole, Sue Amaradivakara and Friederike Huber. Lastly, I should like to thank my dear children, Hugh and Helen Nicholson, for their love and support in difficult times.

Shaftesbury, Dorset, 3 February 2017

Select References

Chapter 1

'An account of Mouswald in the 1790s . . .': Rev Mr Jacob
  Dickson, in *The Statistical Accounts of Scotland 1791–1845*, Old
  Statistical Accounts, vol. VII (Edinburgh, 1793).

Chapter 3

'Snowe is whyght . . .': William Fulke, *A Goodly Gallery with
  a Most Pleasaunt Prospect* (London, 1563), f. 56.
'killing geese in Scotland . . .': quoted by Mary Moorman,
  William Wordsworth: A Biography (Oxford, 1957),
  vol. 1, pp. 10–11.

Chapter 4

'an Englishman called Edmund Burt . . .': Edmund Burt,
  Burt's Letters from the North of Scotland (Edinburgh, 1998),
  pp. 154–7, originally published as *Letters from a Gentleman in
  the North of Scotland to His Friend in London* (London, 1754).
'lumbago, muscular inflammation . . .': Walter Jackson Bate,
  Samuel Johnson (London, 1977), p. 434.
'a considerable protuberance . . .': James Boswell, *The Journal
  of a Tour to the Hebrides* (London, 1786), p. 130.
'Of the hills, which our journey offered . . .': Samuel Johnson,
  A Journey to the Western Isles of Scotland (London, 1775), p. 81.
'sixty days in the winter of 1683–84 . . .': G. Manley, '1684: The
  Coldest Winter in the Instrumental Record', *Weather*, vol.

30, no. 12 (1975).

'seven out of the eight winters between 1693 and 1700 . . .':
M.E. Pearson, 'Two memorable winters in Scotland –
1793/94 and 1794/5', *Weather*, vol. 49, no. 12 (1994).

'One estimate suggests that the snow line . . .': H. Lamb,
Weather, Climate and Human Affairs (London, 1988), p. 158.

'a good few eighteenth-century travellers . . .': Lance Tufnell,
'Summer snow in northern England', *Journal of Meteorology*,
vol. 18, no. 181 (1993).

'rises with precipice over precipice . . .': J. Clarke, *A Survey of
the Lakes of Cumberland, Westmoreland and Lancashire, etc.*
(Penrith and London, 1787).

'to be placed in the midst of a Wood . . .': Thomas Bewick, *A
Memoir of Thomas Bewick, written by himself*, ed. Ian Bain
(Oxford, 1975), p. 81.

'He collected a lump and brought it down . . .': Luke Howard,
The Climate of London (London, 1833), vol. 2, p. 303.

'beside College Burn . . .': G. Scott, 'Lingering snow on
Cheviot', *Weather*, vol. 19, no. 7 (1964), pp. 204–5.

Billy Gilbert: communication to the author from Tim Elliott,
6 November 2006.

Chapter 5

'as much as sixty-five feet . . .': D. Nethersole-Thompson and
A. Watson, *The Cairngorms* (London, 1974), p. 232.

'the tunnel ten feet high . . .': William Forsyth, *In the Shadow of
Cairngorm. Chronicles of the united parishes of Abernethy and
Kincardine* (Inverness, 1900), p. 268.

'a wretched hag . . .': William Forsyth, ibid., p. 268.

'a certain Margaret . . .': *Crerar's Guide to Badenoch*, 6th edition
(1910), p. 73.

'a Glen Feshie maiden . . .': Alexander Inkson McConnochie,

Guide to Aviemore and Vicinity (Aviemore, 1902), p. 48.

'I never saw death look so beautiful . . .': Rev Francis Kilvert, *Kilvert's Diary*, ed. W. Plomer (London, 1940), vol. 3, pp. 441–3.

'There are three smiles worse than sorrow . . .': K. Meyer (ed.), *The Triads of Ireland*, vol. 13 of the Todd Lecture Series of the Royal Irish Academy (Dublin and London, 1913).

Chapter 7

'The poet John Taylor . . .': John Taylor, *The Pennyles Pilgrimage* (London, 1618); Daniel Defoe, *A Tour thro' the Whole Island of Great Britain* (London, 1724–27), Letter XIII, Part 4.

'John Drummond . . .': Adam Watson and Iain Cameron, *Cool Britannia* (Rothersthorpe, 2010), p. 11.

'Accuracy of narration . . .': Samuel Johnson, ibid., p. 63.

'little of perpetual snow . . .': William Wordsworth, *A Description of the Scenery of the Lakes in the North of England* (London, 1822; originally published anonymously as the introduction to J. Wilkinson's *Select Views of Cumberland, Westmoreland, and Lancashire*, 1810).

'one of those fallacies . . .': C.H. Townshend, *A Descriptive Tour in Scotland by T.H.C.* (Brussels, 1840; new edition London, 1846).

'studies of Scottish snowbeds . . .': for example, R.P. Dansey, 'The Glacial Snow of Ben Nevis', *Symons's Meteorological Magazine* (March 1905); R.P. Dansey, 'The Permanent Snow Beds of the Ben Nevis Group', *Symons's Meteorological Magazine* (November 1916); G. Manley, 'Scotland's semi-permanent snows', *Weather*, vol. 26 (1971).

'Mention of glaciers goes back . . .': see Thomas Pennant, *A Tour in Scotland MDCCLXIX* (Chester, 1771), p. 184, for mention of a glacier on Ben Wyvis. In *A Tour in Scotland and*

Voyage to the Hebrides; 1772 (Edinburgh, 1998; first published
Chester, 1774 and 1776), p. 329, Pennant describes 'snowy
glaciers' in the mountains west of Dundonnel, which must
be An Teallach and its neighbouring peaks.
'a 1970s study of lichen growths . . .': D.E. Sugden, 'The
Significance of Periglacial Activity on Some Scottish
Mountains', *The Geographical Journal*, vol. 137 (1971).
'The discussion, occasionally heated...' see Eddie Boyle,
'Perennial snow in the Scottish mountains', http://www.
edwardboyle.com/drupal/snowpatches_resources (no date).

Chapter 8

'Adam Watson . . .': Adam Watson, *It's a Fine Day for the Hill*
(Rothersthorpe, 2011).
'Since the late 1990s, volunteers . . .': the survey is coordinated
by Iain Cameron, who runs a Facebook site on which
people share photos and information, https://en-gb.
facebook.com/groups/snowpatchesscotland.
'a travel guide of 1894 . . .': Murray's *Handbook for Travellers in
Scotland* (London, 1894).
'a vast super-corrie . . .': Adam Watson, *The Cairngorms*
(Edinburgh, 1975), p. 143.
'On the 10th September that year . . .': Seton Gordon,
Highland Days (London, 1963), pp. 23–5.
'the summit of the pass . . .' *Walks and Scrambles in the
Highlands*, Arthur L. Bagley, (London, 1914), p. 30.
'This inner corrie is a very secluded place . . .': James Parker,
Cairngorm Club Journal (1924).
'The snae that lies lang . . .': V.A. Firsoff, *The Cairngorms on
Foot and Ski* (London, 1949).
'A 1974 book on the Cairngorms states . . .': A. Watson and
D. Nethersole-Thompson, ibid., p. 144.

Chapter 9

'ditch vision . . .': Jeremy Hooker, 'Ditch Vision', *Powys Society Journal*, vol. IX (1996).

'holds a forest from the crown . . .': Thomas Pennant, *A Tour in Scotland MDCCLXIX* (Chester, 1771), p. 184.

'a local minister, Harry Robertson . . .': 'Snow on Ben Wyvis', *Ross-shire Journal* (30 June 1950).

'an annual summer rent of a snowball . . .': Seton Gordon, *Highland Days* (London, 1963).

'The Farquharsons were at risk . . .': Adam Watson and Iain Cameron, ibid. p. 26.

'Gladly will I sell . . .': Matsuo Bashō, *The Narrow Road to the Deep North and Other Travel Sketches*, trans. Nobuyuki Yuasa (London, 1966), p. 60.

Andy Goldsworthy: Andy Goldsworthy, *Midsummer Snowballs* (London, 2001).

'My eerie memories . . .': Hugh MacDiarmid, 'The Eemis Stane', from *Collected Poems of Hugh MacDiarmid* (Edinburgh & London, 1962).

Chapter 10

'What can the small violets tell us . . .': William Carlos Williams, 'Raleigh was Right', from *The Collected Poems, Volume II, 1939–1962*, ed. Christopher MacGowan (London, 1988).

Chapter 11

'Kitty's work as an artist . . .': see www.catharinenicholson.com.

'The Snow Party': Derek Mahon, *The Snow Party* (Oxford, 1975).

Hope (2009)
Catharine Nicholson

Photo by Helen Nicholson

About the Author

Christopher Nicholson is the author of three novels,
including *The Elephant Keeper*, which was shortlisted for
the Costa Novel Award and Encore Prize, and *Winter*,
described by Alison Lurie in the *New York Review of Books*
as 'one of the most dramatically convincing and moving
Famous Writer Novels I have ever read.' He has lived near
Shaftesbury in Dorset for the past thirty years.

www.christophernicholsonwriter.com